THE ANCHORED SOUL
Devotional

THE ANCHORED SOUL
Devotional

A Guided 40-Day Devotional
For the overwhelmed, the emotionally
wounded, and the spiritually thirsty: a
space to reflect, and be restored.

Dr. Patricia Hudson-Henry
Founder & Visionary
The Dr. Patricia Wellness Collective™

The Anchored Soul: A 40-Day Devotional
Copyright © 2025 by **Dr. Patricia Hudson-Henry**
All rights reserved.

No part of this book may be reproduced, stored in a retrieval system, or transmitted in any form or by any means—electronic, mechanical, photocopying, recording, or otherwise—without prior written permission from the publisher, except for brief quotations used in reviews, articles, teaching, or sermons.

Published by:
Dr. Patricia Wellness Collective Publishing
Faith-Led. Neuroscience-Based. Heart-Healing.
www.DrPatriciaWellness.com

Cover & Interior Design: Dr. Patricia Wellness Collective
ISBN:979-8-9940032-0-6

Unless otherwise noted, Scripture quotations are taken from the Holy Bible, New King James Version® (NKJV). Scripture quotations marked NIV are taken from THE HOLY BIBLE, NEW INTERNATIONAL VERSION®. Scripture quotations marked NLT are taken from the Holy Bible, New Living Translation®. Scripture quotations marked ESV are from The Holy Bible, English Standard Version®. Scripture quotations marked KJV are from the King James Version. Scripture quotations marked CSB are from the Christian Standard Bible®. Used by permission. All rights reserved. This devotional is intended for spiritual encouragement and personal reflection. It is not a substitute for professional counseling, psychotherapy, or medical care.

Companion Resource:
The Anchored Soul Companion Journal is available as a separate guided reflection tool to deepen your spiritual and emotional journey.
Printed in the United States of America.
 First Printing, 2025.

Dedication

This book is lovingly dedicated to the memory of my baby sister, Blossom Solange Danielle Hudson.

Blossom lived up to her name, beautiful, funny, and full of life. She was a treasured bloom in our family garden: beautiful, brilliant, witty, and unafraid to challenge herself.

Her sudden passing left a silence I cannot explain, a fracture I cannot mend. It hurts. Blossom's life was more than moments of joy. It was a testimony of resilience and compassion. She had a heart that stretched wide for children who were unseen, for women who were silenced, who felt forgotten, for the abused who longed for safety. She carried their hope within her, advocated with her presence, and uplifted them with her words.

In many ways, her life was an anchored soul itself rooted in God, reaching for others, and resilient even in the face of life's storms.

May The Anchored Soul carry forward what Blossom lived so well:

that God's presence is safe,

that love is never wasted,

that healing belongs to the hurting,

and that even in our fragility, beauty still blossoms.

She is missed beyond words.

She is loved beyond measure.

And her light will never fade.

—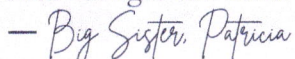

In Loving Memory of Grace Hudson

With deep honor and unending love, I remember my mother, Grace Hudson. Her life was a living testimony of what it means to be an Anchored Soul, steady in faith, unwavering in love, and resilient in storms. She embodied the very principles this devotional carries: rootedness in God, compassion for others, and strength clothed in humility.

Mommy did not just teach me about God's presence; she lived it. She became a safe place for her eight children, the community, and all who crossed her path. Through kindness, courage, and sacrifice, she modeled the anchored living that inspires me to write these words today.

It echoes in every breath I take, in every page of this devotional, in every effort I make to lift the broken, and in every prayer I breathe for the abused, the forgotten, the children, and the women who need to know they are not alone; for fathers who need to learn how to be priests and protectors, and for couples struggling to close the space between them.

Mommy's life was a sermon.

Her love was her anchor.

And her legacy continues through me, through our family, and now through The Anchored Soul community.

— *Patricia*

Acknowledgments

To my husband, Ricardo, thank you for being my steady encourager and for creating sacred space in our marriage for God to do His transforming work through me to elevate others. Thank you for your warm embrace, your love and partnership make this journey possible, and your faith in what God is doing continues to anchor me.

To my children, Ife, Elle-Michelle, and Prince, you remain my living prayers and my greatest joy. May you always know that you are loved and treasured, that your worth is unshakable, and that you are forever anchored in my heart and God's love.

To my siblings, Marion, Ray, Sharon, Cheryl-Ann, Reuben, and Andrea, thank you for walking with me through seasons of loss and love. Together, we carry Mommy's legacy and stand as living proof that love endures. And finally, to my father Carl Hudson, who has taught me that there is a sacred place for forgiveness and healing in our hearts.

Family has been both my anchor and my sail, and I am grateful beyond words. You remind me daily that these words are not just ideas, but living truths. Thank you for receiving this work with open hearts and for becoming witnesses of rest, resilience, and restoration in God.

With deep gratitude and love,
Dr. Patricia Hudson-Henry

Foreword

There comes a point in every life when the waves hit harder than you imagined. When loss leaves you gasping. When shame screams louder than your faith. When even prayer feels like hard work, and your soul whispers, "Lord, God, are You still here?" I wrote this devotional for that moment. For the fragile places we keep hidden from others. For the panic behind your smile, the tears no one hears, and the survival patterns you wish you could change.

It is for the woman who has prayed but still feels overwhelmed.
For those who love Jesus but feel ashamed of the exhaustion.
For every heart that wonders if God is disappointed with their brokenness.
Let me say this plainly: God is not disappointed in you. He is not waiting for you to fix yourself. He draws near to your fragility. His presence is the safest place your soul will ever know. That's why this devotional is called The Anchored Soul. The storms may not stop, but you don't have to drown in them.
You can be anchored. Safe. Held. Loved.

It is a neurospiritual pilgrimage, a meeting place where faith and neuroscience walk together. It is a space where Scripture calms your nervous system and invites your body to rest in what God has already spoken. Where God restores both your theology and your biology. The God who made your soul designed your brain, and He knows how to anchor both.
Across forty days, you will enter a sacred rhythm:
Scripture as your anchor.
Reflections that weave faith and psychology.
Whispers from God for your soul.
Insights from Dr. Patricia.

Throughout Scripture, forty days meant transformation. Moses came down glowing. Jesus emerged ready for the cross. When God sets aside forty days, He rewrites stories. That is my prayer for you. That these forty days would be a divine reset, a sacred re-anchoring. That you will rise radiant, resilient, and restored. You are not too much, too late, or too broken. You are beloved. You are seen. You are safe. You are Loved.
So come as you are: weary, hopeful, fragmented, reaching. God is already here, whispering, "You don't have to hold it all together. Let Me hold you."

Welcome to the journey.
— Dr. Patricia Hudson Henry

SCRIPTURE PERMISSIONS PAGE

Unless otherwise noted, Scripture quotations are taken from the New King James Version® (NKJV).
Copyright © 1982 by Thomas Nelson. Used by permission. All rights reserved.

Scripture quotations marked NIV are taken from the
Holy Bible, New International Version®, NIV®.
Copyright © 1973, 1978, 1984, 2011 by Biblica, Inc.™
Used by permission. All rights reserved worldwide.

Scripture quotations marked ESV are from the
Holy Bible, English Standard Version® (ESV).
Copyright © 2001 by Crossway, a publishing ministry of Good News Publishers.
Used by permission. All rights reserved.

Scripture quotations marked NLT are from the
Holy Bible, New Living Translation (NLT).
Copyright © 1996, 2004, 2015 by Tyndale House Foundation.
Used by permission of Tyndale House Publishers, Inc., Carol Stream, Illinois 60188.
All rights reserved.

Scripture quotations marked CSB are from the
Christian Standard Bible® (CSB).
Copyright © 2017, 2020 by Holman Bible Publishers.
Used by permission. Christian Standard Bible® and CSB® are federally registered trademarks of Holman Bible Publishers.

Scripture marked KJV is from the King James Version, which is in the public domain.

Table of Contents

WEEK 1 ANCHORED IN GOD'S PRESENCE
1

Day 1: The Place that Holds You
Day 2: Beneath the Shadow
Day 3: Come Home to Me
Day 4: The Still Waters Within
Day 5: A Whispers in the Weary Wind
Day 6: Resting Without Earning
Day 7: He Knows Your Frame

WEEK 2 ANCHORED IN IDENTITY
17

Day 8: Even Here, I Am
Day 9: The Place That Holds You
Day 10: The Weight You Can Lay Down
Day 11: Peace Be Still (Inside Me)
Day 12: Crushed but Not Cursed
Day 13: Let This Mind Be in You
Day 14: What If It's Just Too Much?

WEEK 3 ANCHORED IN HEALING
33

Day 15: God's Not Ashamed of Your Tears
Day 16: When Shame Whispers
Day 17: Not Anxious. Anchored
Day 18: The Voice That Calms the Spiral
Day 19: You're Still in the Story
Day 20: When Healing Looks Like Release
Day 21: It's Okay to Say You're Not Okay

WEEK 4 ANCHORED IN SURRENDER
49

Day 22: The Hardest Place to Worship From
Day 23: Faith While You're Still Bleeding
Day 24: Held in the Breaking

Table of Contents

Day 25: When Trust is a Tremble, Not a Roar
Day 26: He sees the Trauma You Don't Speak
Day 27: What Happens When You Don't Feel Spiritual
Day 28: You Are Not a Burden, You Belong

WEEK 5 ANCHORED IN STRENGTH
65
Day 29: You Are Not What You Have Been Through
Day 30: He Calls You His Own.
Day 31: Chosen with a Purpose
Day 32: There is a Gift in Your Sensitivity
Day 33: Loving Without Losing Yourself
Day 34: You Are Not Behind
Day 35: The Voice That Calls You Royal

WEEK 6 ANCHORED IN MISSION
81
Day 36: You're Not Just Healing, You're Being Prepared
Day 37: You Can Build from Here
Day 38: The Rise is Still Holy
Day 39: You're Allowed to Feel Joy Again
Day 40: You've Been Crowned

A FINAL WORD FROM DR. PATRICIA
94
WAYS TO USE THE ANCHORED SOUL DEVOTIONAL & JOURNAL
96
CONNECT WITH DR. PATRICIA
98
ABOUT THE AUTHOR
100

WEEK 1: Anchored in God's Presence

SCRIPTURE ANCHOR

"He who dwells in the secret place of the Most High shall abide under the shadow of the Almighty."

—Psalm 91:1 *(NKJV)*

There is a place that holds you when nothing else can.
A place where panic is met with compassion,
shame cannot speak your name,
and silence becomes safety instead of distance.
God's presence is that place. It isn't withheld from you; it was prepared for you.
This first week invites you to rediscover safety by letting your nervous system release its tension and remembering that God never asks you to perform.
You simply come as you are.
Here, you'll discover that His shadow isn't dark, it's shelter.
His stillness isn't empty. It's restoration.
His whisper isn't fragile. It's power.
This is the week you dwell in His presence.
It is the week you settle into the sanctuary that doesn't move when life does.
By the end of it, you won't just believe God is with you;
you'll begin to feel it in your heart.

DAY 1

The Place That Holds You

SCRIPTURE ANCHOR

"He who dwells in the secret place of the Most High shall abide under the shadow of the Almighty."
—Psalm 91:1 (NKJV)

There is a place where your panic doesn't disqualify you.
Where your survival responses don't shame you.
Where your tears need no translation,
and your silence isn't distance.
It is called the secret place of the Most High.
Not hidden from you, hidden for you, friend.

A sanctuary for the dysregulated,
a refuge for the raw hurt,
a shelter for the ones still trying to hold it together.
I have known what it is to live inside a body that bends beneath its own weight, yet still be held by His grace.
There were seasons when even sitting upright felt like faith,
when discomfort pulsed louder and heavier than prayer.

And still, in that secret place, He whispers,
you are not failing, you are healing.
Every breath that reaches for Me is worship,
every tremble that leans toward hope is faith.

You are not behind, you are becoming.
Growing and becoming the beauty you were made to be.
That secret place taught me this:
stability is not the absence of our struggles;
it is the absolute assurance of His Presence.

This isn't just a metaphor; it's a **neurospiritual** safe place.
Where your mind unclenches, your body learns it's no longer in danger,
and your soul rests quietly, not because the storm stopped,
but because you found the shelter inside it.
You don't have to earn this place. You have to come.
The secret place isn't found by striving,
but by surrendering to the One who already made room for you.

So come empty if you must.
Come trembling if you need to.
But come because the secret place doesn't demand your perfection,
 it invites your presence.
And when you arrive, you'll find that He's been waiting all along,
not with questions about your strength,
but with arms wide enough to hold your storm and your surrender in the same embrace.

Whisper from God
"Come home, My beloved. Come to the place where your worth isn't measured by strength.
Where I don't ask you to perform or be perfect.
Where I won't flinch at your fear or fold at your sadness.
You can rest here with Me, you're already under My shadow."
~ *Love, God*

DR. PATRICIA SAYS...
*"The nervous system needs more than truth, it needs safety.
And the secret place is where spiritual safety
and emotional regulation meet.
You don't have to fix yourself first, my sister,
the place that holds you is already open and warm."*

DAY 2

Beneath the Shadow

SCRIPTURE ANCHOR

"He will cover you with His feathers, and under His wings you will find refuge; His faithfulness will be your shield and rampart."
—Psalm 91:4 (NIV)

There's a quiet kind of safety here, not the kind that demands silence,
but the kind that gives you permission to exhale:
to cry, to free yourself from heartache, loss, and pain.
And for you to be covered without explanation.
Being beneath His shadow isn't weakness; it's co-regulation with the Divine.
In trauma healing, we teach that safety isn't only physical, it's physiological.
Your nervous system needs a signal that says:
You're not alone anymore.
You're safe now.
You can settle. Be happy. Allow love in.

God's wings aren't decorative; they're functional and regulatory,
they are an emotional armor made of His presence.
He covers. He shields. He speaks peace without performance.
I have felt this covering through my sisters who prayed with me in our grief,
laughed me back to life in the moments sadness took hold.
They refused to let despair have the last word.

Their love has been God's wings in human form,
reminding me that divine shelter often arrives through earthly arms.
There's something holy about being held when you can't hold yourself.
The body remembers what the mind forgets. Touch, empathy, and presence
are all languages God speaks fluently through His people.
In those moments, I realized healing doesn't always look miraculous;
it may look like someone staying beside you when you have no words left.

This is the beginning of **_Emotional Disrobing_™:**
the vulnerable act of taking off your armor of pride, perfection, sadness, and shame,
and being seen without defense.
It takes courage to be uncovered before God,
to let Him see the trembling and the truth at the same time.
But every layer you release becomes space for grace to breathe.
And in that surrender, your nervous system learns what your spirit already knew:
You are safe here. You are home.
You don't need to manage your image here.
You don't need to explain your triggers, those things that always get to you.
Just let the uncovering work, so His covering can work.

Whisper from God
Come close. I won't rush you. I won't shame you
for the armor you've worn.
But here, under My wings, you don't have to wear it anymore.
You are safe with Me. Rest beneath My shadow.
I'll cover what you've had to protect for far too long.
~Love, God

DR. PATRICIA SAYS...
"Stillness isn't passivity, it's permission.
Beneath God's shadow, thriving begins when the survival brain softens,
the heart exhales, and the body remembers: I'm safe now. That's when healing begins."

DAY 3

Come Home to Me

SCRIPTURE ANCHOR

"Come to Me, all you who are weary and burdened, and I will give you rest."
—Matthew 11:28 (NIV)

There's a kind of tired that sleep can't fix.
It lives in the bones, in the nervous system,
in the places that have been on high alert far too long.
That's the kind of tired Jesus speaks to and wants to heal.
I think of the quiet hours when my children were small and sleep was
inconsistent…study hours were long, and my body was weary,
My mommy's mind was racing with concerns about managing time, coping
with exhaustion and maintaining a heavenly harmony in our home.

In those moments, rest felt impossible until I learned that surrender
is not giving up, it is letting God parent me,
while I parent the little treasures He gave me.
He does not say, "Fix yourself, then come."
He says, "Come as you are, weary, heavy, carrying too much."

This is rest for your nervous system, the quieting of inner chaos,
a homecoming for the soul.
So many live stuck in The Limiting Loop™, patterns of emotional survival:
over-explaining, withdrawing, controlling, pleasing, shutting down.
These are not moral failings; they are your protective reflexes from life
experiences that taught you: seek survival first, and find connection later.
But in the presence of Jesus, the Lord, you do not have to perform.
You do not have to explain why you are exhausted.
You do not even need to find the right words.
You just have to come.

There is a rhythm to divine rest.
It begins with release and ends with renewal.
When you finally stop fighting your fatigue and lean into His arms,
you'll notice your breath deepen, your shoulders drop,
and your mind begins to unclench from the need to control outcomes.
This is what restoration feels like: sacred exhale.

Rest doesn't mean absence of responsibility.
It means His presence within it.
You can still lead, nurture, and serve from a heart that is regulated.
When grace becomes your pace, peace becomes your posture.

And the same God who sustains galaxies
can sustain your nervous system, too.
And when you do, you'll find more than relief, you'll find rest.
Real, restoring rest, the kind that rewires your **Limiting Loop™**.

Whisper from God
Come home to Me, beloved. Let Me be the soft landing your soul has searched for.
I know how long you have been carrying this.
What no one sees, I see. What no one hears, I hear.
You do not have to figure it all out.
Just come. I'll give you rest, your mind doesn't have to earn.
— Love, God

DR. PATRICIA SAYS...
"The Limiting Loop™ keeps us stuck in protection instead of connection.
Rest rewires the loop.
Rest is resistance that breaks the loop, and in God's presence, it becomes recovery."

DAY 4

The Still Waters Within

SCRIPTURE ANCHOR

"He leads me beside still waters; He restores my soul."
—Psalm 23:2–3 (NIV)

Sometimes your life looks calm on the outside,
but inside, you are rushing like rapids,
the pressure to keep it all together,
the unresolved pain you have pushed down,
the tension in your body that refuses to release.
It can feel as though peace is for other people, but not for you.
Yet God does not only calm the storms around you—
He quiets the ones within you. Hallelujah!

In Psalm 23, "still waters" are more than a scenic image.
They symbolize internal regulation, the sacred moment when your nervous
system stops scanning for danger and begins to trust safety.
That is where the foundation of healing is laid:
in regulated safety, not forced serenity.

Many people attempt to achieve peace through orchestrated performance,
checking spiritual boxes, silencing feelings, or striving harder to "have faith."
However, performance will never produce the restoration your soul craves.

This is where **Emotional Echo™** becomes essential:
your body may still respond to past chaos,
even when your present feels peaceful.
That does not mean you are faithless,
it means your healing is still unfolding.
Even forgiveness or apology is only the beginning;
true healing is an internal rewiring that takes time.

where peace is not a prize to earn, but a Presence to encounter.
The Shepherd is not asking for your perfection;
He is inviting your participation in the slowing, the softening, the staying.
In His company, even your trembling becomes worship.

When your inner waters begin to still, your outer world will start to reflect it.
Peace will no longer feel foreign; it will feel familiar.
And the same God who speaks to oceans speaks to your body too,
saying, "Be still, beloved. You are safe now."

Whisper from God
It is finished, beloved.
You don't have to carry what I already covered.
You don't have to earn what I already gave.
I'm not watching your performance, I'm holding your heart.
Can you lay off the pressure?
Let Me show you what rest feels like when it's rooted in love, not fear.
— Love, God

DR. PATRICIA SAYS...
"Stillness isn't only spiritual, it's biological.
It's what your nervous system longs for.
Emotional Echo™ reminds us that the past can shout
loudly in the present,
but still waters are where the echo softens,
and God restores what's been scattered."

DAY 5

A Whisper in the Weary Wind

SCRIPTURE ANCHOR

"And after the earthquake a fire, but the Lord was not in the fire; and after the fire, a still small voice."
—1 Kings 19:12 (NKJV)

Elijah had just called down fire from heaven, outrun a chariot, and faced hundreds of false prophets.
But after the victory came his big crash.
Fear, fatigue, and despair washed over him.
His amygdala was overwhelmed, prefrontal reasoning dimmed, and he ran.

You don't have to be in a spiritual drought to feel empty.
Sometimes it's after your greatest outpouring that you feel most alone.
And like Elijah, you may whisper, "Where is God now?"
But God didn't appear in the drama.
He wasn't in the wind, the earthquake, or the fire.
He came in a whisper, a still, small voice that did not demand but invited.

That's how the nervous system heals, too, not through force, but through safety. His whisper tells your body, It's safe to slow down.
Safe to come out of hiding. Safe to be held without hustling.

Many high-performing believers remain trapped in the echo of fight-or-flight.
The drive to achieve more, to do greater things for God, can sometimes become louder than His love.
But God does not shout over your survival brain.
He would like to speak to your regulated one.
This is the holy work of internal re-patterning,
where adrenaline gives way to rest,
and achievement makes room for connection.

Sometimes, the greatest miracle isn't fire from heaven,
it's calm within your chest.
It's learning to worship without urgency,
to serve without self-erasure,
to let your nervous system believe what your spirit already knows:
that God is not only mighty, He is gentle.

There were moments when the world tried to limit my progress,
when doors closed without reason and expectations pressed heavily.
But like Elijah, I found that God's whisper still called me forward,
reminding me that no human ceiling can contain a God-ordained assignment.

And maybe that's what the wilderness is for:
not punishment, but recalibration.
A place where God detoxes your pace and resets your priorities.
Where you learn that His presence is not earned through movement, but encountered in stillness, Elijah didn't need another mission. He needed a moment with God. And so do you.

Whisper from God
I don't need you to prove anything.
I'm not in the noise of your performance or the pressure of success.
I'm here, in the whisper.
I see your effort, but now I want to restore your energy.
Lay down your sword, just for a moment, and let Me speak where you're tired.
— Love, God

DR. PATRICIA SAYS...

"Elijah ran from the threat, but God reintroduced safety.
That's the healing work, helping your brain unlearn the lie that noise equals power.
Sometimes the most powerful moment is the whisper that says, "You can come out now. You're safe."

DAY 6

Resting Without Earning

SCRIPTURE ANCHOR

"Come to me, all you who are weary and burdened, and I will give you rest. Take my yoke upon you and learn from me, for I am gentle humble in heart, and you will find rest for your souls."
—Matthew 11:28–29 (NIV)

These were the words of Jesus, an invitation extended to us, not an instruction. "Come to Me."
Not when you have it together,
not when the list is done,
not when the mask feels lighter.
Come as you are, tired, anxious, overextended, and still worthy of rest.

Yet so many of us are still trying to earn our way into peace.
We have spiritualized striving.
We pray from panic. We serve from depletion.
And we wonder why we still feel as though we are drowning beneath the weight of not enough. Our spiritual gifts, meant to bring joy, now bringing weariness and fatigue.

I understand that kind of exhaustion, the kind that grows from responsibility, from being the one who felt she had to do all the things and do them well. As a wife, a mother, a sister, and a daughter of the Caribbean, I learned early how to keep going, to make it happen, and still look polished.
But survival can start to feel necessary
when you forget that rest is needed, too.
This, beloved, is the lingering remnant,
when the nervous system confuses rest with danger.
A lingering remnant isn't only what happened to you;
it's what happened within you as a result.

It is the body's memory of overwhelm, the way your system learned to stay alert long after the threat was gone.
When you have lived in survival mode for too long, stillness can feel unfamiliar, even unsafe.
That is why we keep moving, fixing, and performing, even for God.

But hear this, beloved: Jesus did not only die to forgive your sin, He died to restore your safety. This is a hallelujah moment!!!

So queens,
You can rest because the cross removed your need to hustle for worth.
You can breathe because you are no longer trapped in the Limiting Loop™ of over-functioning.
You can stop proving, because heaven already said "yes" to you.
Rest is not a reward for spiritual productivity.
It is your birthright as a beloved child of God.

Whisper from God
It is finished, beloved.
You don't have to carry what I already covered.
You don't have to earn what I already gave.
I'm not watching your performance, I'm holding your heart.
Lay down the pressure.
Let Me show you what rest feels like when it's rooted in love, not fear.
— Love, God

DR. PATRICIA SAYS...
"When your nervous system is used to survival mode, rest feels like risk. But safety isn't found in doing more — it's found in trusting the finished work.
Rest isn't lazy. Rest is recovery.
It's the place where your body learns what your spirit already knows:
You're safe.
Today, my heart says, 'I need rest.' How about you?"

DAY 7

He Knows Your Frame

SCRIPTURE ANCHOR

"For He knows our frame; He remembers that we are dust."
—Psalm 103:14 (ESV)

There are moments when your strength runs out,
when you forget the verse, drop the ball,
or feel as though you are failing at faith.
But God never forgets your frame.
After all, He created it.

He does not expect you to be steel when He designed you from dust.
This verse is not a rebuke; it is a reminder. God does not misread your limits,
and He is never confused about your limitations.
He made you with intention.
He knows your biology, your brain, your wiring, and your trauma history.
He responds with compassion, not criticism.

I think about growing up in Trinidad,
a life filled with adventure, climbing fruit trees, playing marble pitch,
hearing the laughter of my seven siblings, and living within the unspoken
rhythm of resilience. We learned early to be present for each other when life
grew heavy, protect one another, to share, to sacrifice, to seek excellence,
and to worship.

But I also learned that strength can be a perfect hiding place for fatigue,
and that sometimes the bravest thing you can do is to stop pretending to be
strong. That same resilience followed me into adulthood, into classrooms,
hospitals, and conference halls.
As a professor and clinician, I've spent twenty-four plus years teaching others
about emotional regulation,

about how faith and neuroscience meet in the body's design for healing.
I created programs to help others rest, reconnect, and recover, and yet, somewhere between purpose and pressure, I forgot how to pause myself.
I became so practiced at being strong that my nervous system began to believe it was normal. Only now, with a doctor's note in hand and permission to rest, am I remembering that restoration is holy work too.
The healer also needs healing. The teacher also needs tending.

When your nervous system reaches overload, your reactions may not look "spiritual." You might withdraw, snap, cry, say unkind things, or shut down. That is not rebellion. It is your body sounding the alarm that God Himself designed within your brain. And God hears that alarm, too.

He does not measure you by how perfectly you hold it together.
He meets you in your fragile, fractured frame and says, I am still here. I still want you. This is grace at a cellular level, where your story, your biology, and your spirit meet, and God chooses to love you right there,
in the dust and in the brokenness.

Whisper from God

Beloved, I remember how I made you.
I know what you carry and how it has stretched you.
I'm not frustrated by your fatigue.
I'm not surprised by your fragility.
I'm not disappointed in your process.
Let Me hold you, not the version of you that "gets it right," but the version that just needs to breathe.
— Love, God

DR. PATRICIA SAYS...

"God's mercy is trauma-informed.
He knows your frame, the way stress and fear have shaped your nervous system.
You are not broken.
You are beloved. You are healing.
Dust is not a flaw, it's the starting point of grace."

WEEK 2: Anchored in Identity

SCRIPTURE ANCHOR

"Do not fear, for I have redeemed you; I have called you by name; you are mine."

—Isaiah 43:1 *(NKJV)*

Before you can walk in freedom, you must know who you are. Trauma renames you — too much, not enough, unclean, unworthy. But healing whispers your true name: Daughter. Beloved. Royal, Mine. This week calls you back to identity. You'll see that you are not your shame, not your spiral, not your survival role. You are Chosen. Called. Seen.

I know what it is to be renamed by pain, to carry the weight of being the strong one, the safe one, the one who holds everyone else together. But I've also learned that identity is not performance, it's Presence. It's remembering that who you are in God cannot be stolen by what happened to you. Even when your hands still tremble, even when your soul still questions, God's voice overrules the lies and says: "You are Mine."

By the end of this week, you will begin to rise differently, not because your circumstances changed, but because your identity did.

DAY 8

Even Here, I Am

SCRIPTURE ANCHOR

"My Presence will go with you, and I will give you rest."
—EXODUS 33:14 (NIV)

These words were first spoken to Moses,
a leader overwhelmed by responsibility,
standing between a weary people and an uncertain future.
God did not promise him a map,
but, His Presence. Sometimes rest feels impossible
not because your schedule is full,
but because your soul is on guard.

You are not merely tired; you are hyper-aware,
scanning for what might go wrong,
waiting for the next disappointment,
rehearsing how to respond if things fall apart.

That vigilance once kept you safe.
It is how your brain learned to survive, to stay alert, to feel secure.
But into that constant watchfulness God speaks softly:
Even here, I am.

You do not have to escape your circumstances to find His Presence.
You do not have to regulate yourself before you receive His rest.
He comes into the tense places, the anxious mornings,
and the tear-soaked pillows,
and He whispers peace.

When I was a girl growing up in Trinidad, surrounded by seven siblings in a house always full of motion and sound,
I learned early how to listen for calm beneath the noise.

Maybe that was where God began training my spirit to find stillness and to observe others. I was always a quiet child, hiding, listening, observing, and He was there with me.

Now I understand: this is co-regulation with God,
the slowing of breath and heart rate that happens when your nervous system senses you are no longer alone.
His Presence is not only spiritual; it is soothing.
His nearness is not abstract theology; it is neurological safety.

And when the noise of life rises again,
emails, deadlines, expectations, and unseen pressures,
He doesn't withdraw; He adjusts His rhythm to mine.
He sits with me in the overwhelm until my heart catches His cadence.
This is the miracle of Presence:
not escape from chaos, but communion within it.

This is not about feeling peaceful; it's about learning that He's with you even when you don't feel peace at all. You are not forgotten or ignored. You are not abandoned or disowned. You are not too complicated. Even here, especially here, He is.

Whisper from God

You don't need to reach for Me; I am already near.
I am not waiting for the storm to end before I comfort you.
I am here in the mess, the tension, and the not-yet-healed places.
My Presence will not add pressure; it will lift it.
I am your rest. Even here.
~ Love, God

DR. PATRICIA SAYS...

"Hypervigilance is a trauma reflex, your brain's effort to keep you safe. But co-regulation is a healing reflex. God's presence is the safest co-regulator there is. You don't have to come out of survival mode alone. He comes to find you inside it, and leads you out gently. His presence is regulated, breathe within and begin to feel his powerful peaceful presence."

DAY 9

The Place That Holds You

SCRIPTURE ANCHOR

"Do not be anxious about anything, but in every situation, by prayer and petition, with thanksgiving, present your requests to God. And the peace of God, which transcends all understanding, will guard your hearts and your minds in Christ Jesus."
—Phillipians 4:6-7 (NIV)

Anxiety does not always announce itself.
It slips in through racing thoughts, shallow breathing,
or overfunctioning that looks like competence.
Sometimes it hides in exhaustion,
in replaying every word you said,
in wondering why you cannot simply calm down.

Sometimes, it sounds like the whisper that says,
If I stop, everything will fall apart.
But here is what many people do not understand:
you cannot pray your way out of a dysregulated nervous system
if your body does not also feel safe.
That is not a lack of faith; it is biology.
And God, who made your brain, understands both.

His peace guards your heart and your mind
because He knows both need protection,
not only your theology, but your physiology.
Not only your beliefs, but your biology.
God does not only want your praise, He wants your panic.
He is not irritated by your overthinking.
He knows how deeply it is connected to your pain, your past, and your
protection patterns. I have felt this too.

Before speaking at conferences or preaching,
my heart races, and I feel overwhelmed by the responsibility
to speak biblical truths clearly and faithfully.
My mind begins to spin faster than my *'peace'* can catch up.
In those moments, I have learned to pause,
to breathe deeply, to notice what is happening in my body,
and to invite God into my physiology, not just my prayers.
Without fail, peace arrives,
not as a flood, but as a gentle guard around my mind.

This is what I call the **Divine Flow:**
1. Bring your anxious thoughts to God honestly.
2. Wrap them in gratitude, not to fake joy, but to anchor in reality.
3. Receive peace that does not make sense, yet does its job: guarding you.

The situation may not change,
but His Presence changes you within it.
Peace may not explain itself,
but it will sustain you.

Whisper from God
You don't have to silence your thoughts before I draw near.
I'm here, even while your mind spins.
Bring it to Me not polished, not processed: just as it is.
I am the Peace that will hold you when you feel like you're unraveling.
— Love, God

DR. PATRICIA SAYS...

"Anxiety isn't just in your head, it's in your body. When you combine honesty with gratitude, your nervous system begins to reorient. That's when peace becomes a protector, not a performance."

DAY 10

The Weight You Can Lay Down

SCRIPTURE ANCHOR

"Cast all your anxiety on Him because He cares for you."
— 1 Peter 5:7 (NIV)

Anxiety does not always feel like fear.
Sometimes it looks like responsibility,
like carrying everyone's needs
and bracing for the next wave.
Like thinking, if I do not hold it together, it will all fall apart.

But here is the truth: you were never designed to carry it all.
This verse does not tell you to ignore your anxiety;
it invites you to cast it.
And the Greek word for cast means to throw forcefully,
to surrender it completely,
not to gently place it down while keeping one cautious eye on it.

In Trinidad, we would say, "Do not give it a kokey eye."
Do not half-release your worries while still watching to see what happens.
Throw it. Let it go.

That is hard for the strong ones,
the mothers, leaders, and fixers who carry worlds on their backs.
I know what that feels like.
I have lived with the tension of being a safe place for others
while secretly asking, But who holds me?

Here is the liberating truth: casting your care is not weakness;
it is attachment.
Asking to be held is not selfish.

You are not failing for finally saying, This is too much.
Casting your care is not avoidance; it is an act of attachment to God.
It is allowing your burdened nervous system to transfer weight into a place of safety.

It is co-regulation with the One who never drops what you give Him.
You can be assured of this:
you are transferring the weight from your nervous system
into the hands of a faithful God.
You do not have to hold it all today:
not in your body,
not in your mind,
not in your spirit.

Whisper from God
"You're not built to carry this alone, beloved.
I see how tightly you're holding it all together.
Let it fall into My hands, all of it.
I'm not shocked by your struggle; your trust moves me.
When you cast your cares, you cast your heart,
and I always catch both."
— *Love, God*

DR. PATRICIA SAYS...
"You're not weak for having a limit — you're wise for identifying it and honoring it. Casting your anxiety is more than a verse, it is a nervous system intervention and prerogative. Healing begins when you finally believe you're safe enough to set it down."

DAY 11

Peace, Be Still (Inside Me)

SCRIPTURE ANCHOR

"Then He arose and rebuked the wind, and said to the sea, 'Peace, be still!' And the wind ceased and there was a great calm."
—Mark 4:39 (NKJV)

You have probably heard this story before: Jesus asleep in the boat while the disciples panicked in the storm.
But perhaps today the storm is not outside; it is inside.

It hides behind your polished exterior,
the smile, the clothes, the warm words spoken to others.
Hidden behind are waves of overthinking,
a constant swirl of what ifs and why nows,
thunderclaps of fear,
and swells of exhaustion and self-doubt.

Jesus did not wake to explain the storm.
He did not offer a plan or express disappointment.
He did not unpack their trauma history or provide a five-point strategy.
He stood in the chaos and said, "Peace, be still."

The same Jesus who speaks to oceans speaks to your inner storm:
to your spinning thoughts,
your pounding heart,
Your nervous system is locked in a fight-or-flight response.

"Peace, be still" is not only a biblical moment; it is a biological miracle.
When you hear His voice in the storm, your amygdala, the brain's fear center, begins to quiet.

Your body shifts from fight-or-flight to rest-and-restore.
Your vagus nerve, the body's pathway of calm, activates and sends signals of safety throughout your entire being.
That is the power of divine co-regulation.
That is neurotheology in motion.
That is peace that does not wait for perfect conditions.

And no, it does not always happen instantly.
Sometimes the storm outside still rages.
But when the internal sea grows calm, you begin to realize this truth:
Peace is not the absence of chaos.
Peace is the presence of Jesus within it.

I have lived with disappointment from failure, with hurt, with missed opportunities, and with the weight of responsibility that comes from standing between storms for others.
Yet I have also seen how His voice still reaches into my inner tempest, steadying my soul when my own strength falters.

Whisper from God
"I see the storm in you, not just around you.
And I'm not afraid to step into it.
My voice still carries authority.
I speak to the wind and the waves,
and I speak to the fear in your chest.
Peace. Be still.
I'm not leaving the boat. I'm here, with power and tenderness."
— Love, God

DR. PATRICIA SAYS...
"When your nervous system is flooded,
you don't need more logic, you need presence.
Jesus' voice is your spiritual vagus nerve reset.
Let His words travel through you until your breath remembers:
peace is still possible."

DAY 12

Crushed but Not Cursed

SCRIPTURE ANCHOR

"The Lord is close to the brokenhearted and saves those who are crushed in spirit."
—Psalm *34:18* (NKJV)

There is a kind of pain that cannot be explained.
It does not always carry visible wounds or dramatic stories.
Sometimes it is the slow ache of being unseen, unheard, or unchosen.

The psalmist calls it being crushed in spirit, that deep-down breaking where hope leaks out and joy feels unreachable.
Even within the walls of faith, this can happen.
We have a name for it: church hurt.

But here is the promise: God comes closer in the crushing.
Not symbolically, but somatically.
He does not wait for your spirit to bounce back;
He draws near to the collapse.

When your nervous system begins to shut down, what psychologists call hypoarousal, God does not step back; He leans in.
He meets you in the numbness, the detachment, and the exhaustion.
He meets you when you have been unseen, mistreated, or ignored.

You are not cursed because you feel crushed.
You are not weak because you cannot "just get over it."
You are not broken beyond repair or wounded beyond healing.
You are precisely the kind of person this verse was written for.

I have felt overlooked and overworked,
carrying the quiet burden of being taken for granted

While holding my own invisible, 'Why's.'
In those seasons, God did not shame my frailty;
He sat with me in it.

And here is what I learned in the silence between my prayers,
God does His deepest work in the places others dismiss.
He gathers every tear they ignore,
holds every ache they minimize,
and rebuilds identities quietly shattered by careless hands.
What people break in haste, God restores with tenderness.

Even when no one sees your private pain, God does.
Even when no one knows what it took to get out of bed, God does.
Even when one sees those who hurt you walk in denial, God does.
Even when others minimize your story, God does not.
 …And even when your spirit whispers, "I cannot do this again,"
God answers, "You do not have to do it alone."

Whisper from God
"I am not distant from your pain; I dwell in it with you.
You don't have to be strong enough to summon Me.
I see the tears behind your smile,
the silence behind your yes, the ache you hide.
I am not walking away from your crushed places, I'm healing them
with My presence."
—: Love, God

DR. PATRICIA SAYS…
"Crushed in spirit isn't the end of the story,
it's where divine proximity begins.
Even when your nervous system shuts down,
God doesn't withdraw.
That's when healing starts, not when you're strong again,
but when you're safe enough to be soft."

DAY 13

Let This Mind Be in You

SCRIPTURE ANCHOR

"Let this mind be in you, which was also in Christ Jesus."
—Philippians 2:5 (KJV)

There is a quiet battle inside your mind every day,
not only between good and evil,
but between fear and trust,
shame and worthiness,
survival and surrender.

Your thoughts do not merely shape your theology;
they shape your biology.
Your brain rewires itself according to the thoughts you rehearse
and the emotions you reinforce.
That is neuroplasticity:
science catching up to Scripture's timeless truth:
your mind can be renewed.

But here is what is beautiful.
The verse does not command you to force the mind of Christ.
It says, "Let this mind be in you." It is an invitation.
It is surrender, not striving. You do not achieve it; you allow it.
What a miracle of mercy that transformation begins with permission,
not performance.

You allow the mindset of Jesus to interrupt your inner critic.
You allow the calm authority of Christ
to speak when anxiety tries to take over.
You allow gentleness to take the place of harsh self-judgment.

This is where trauma-trained reactions are met by Christ-trained peace, and where survival instincts slowly give way to sacred instincts of rest. Peace becomes your default, not your performance.

I think of my own journey:
living with scoliosis and the physical awareness of limitation,
navigating the ache of my parents' separation,
and learning to mother with both strength and softness.
Each of these seasons invited me to let His mind reshape mine.
And in the quiet work of renewal,
I discovered that the mind of Christ is not a distant ideal,
it is a daily companionship,
a gentle re-patterning of thought and emotion
until peace begins to think through you.

Whisper from God
"I'm not asking you to control your thoughts,
I'm inviting you to yield them.
My mind is full of truth,
tenderness, clarity, and peace.
You don't have to chase perfection,
just let Me renew the way you see yourself and others.
Even when your thoughts turn against you,
Mine toward you remains love."
— Love, God

DR. PATRICIA SAYS...
"Neuroplasticity is proof that God designed us for healing.
Letting the mind of Christ in is a neurological reset.
When fear circuits quiet and compassion circuits grow,
you're not just thinking differently,
you're living from a different place."

DAY 14

What If It's Just Too Much?

SCRIPTURE ANCHOR

*"So do not fear, for I am with you;
do not be dismayed, for I am your God.
I will strengthen you and help you;
I will uphold you with my righteous right hand."*
—Isaiah 41:10 (NKJV)

Some days faith feels like a whisper.
Your body is tired, your thoughts are heavy,
and your prayers sound like sighs.
You look at the responsibilities, the family you are protecting,
the calling you are carrying, and you whisper,
"What if this is just too much?"

God never shames that question.
He meets it with a promise,
not that life will be easy,
but that He will hold you through it.

When your nervous system says, "I am overwhelmed,"
God says, "I am with you."
When your capacity feels limited and your resilience feels gone,
He does not demand that you dig deeper;
He lends His strength.

This is a trauma-informed promise:
you do not have to regulate this moment alone.
You do not have to hold yourself up by willpower.
You can lean.

In neuroscience, we call it co-regulation:
the way one steady presence calms another.
Spiritually, it is the righteous right hand
that steadies you when yours begin to tremble.

I have leaned on that hand many times,
when motherhood stretched me,
when professional doors closed and glass ceilings felt too high,
when I depended on my sisters' prayers
and my husband's quiet strength.
Each time, God upheld me,
reminding me that I was never too much for Him.

That same steady Presence is offered to you,
a regulated, righteous hand to hold you
when yours are trembling.
When it feels too much, do not hide. Reach!

Whisper from God
"Beloved, I see what you're carrying.
I know what it's costing you to hold it all together.
You are not a burden.
You are not too much.
And this moment is not too much for Me.
Lean into My strength, I've got you.
— Love, God"

DR. PATRICIA SAYS...
"Your nervous system recognizes limit
long before your mind admits it.
What feels like weakness
is often an invitation to co-regulation.
God is the most faithful co-regulator
you will ever know.
Strength isn't pretending, it's reaching."

WEEK 3: Anchored in Healing

SCRIPTURE ANCHOR

"He heals the brokenhearted and binds up their wounds."

—Psalm 147:3 (NKJV)

Healing is holy, but it rarely feels glamorous.
It looks like tears that won't stop.
Memories that still sting.
Shame that sneaks back louder than faith.
But every fragile moment is sacred ground,
because God bends low to meet you there.
This week is about allowing God into the raw places,
the tears, the spirals, the "I'm not okay."
You will learn that your nervous system is not your enemy,
that grief is not weakness,
and that shame is not your name.
Healing doesn't mean skipping the valley.
It means discovering that Jesus walks into it, whispering:
"No condemnation. Only compassion."
By the end of this week, you will know that your broken places are not the end of your story. They are the beginning of restoration.

DAY 15

God's Not Ashamed of Your Tears

SCRIPTURE ANCHOR

"Jesus wept."
—John 11:35 (NKJV)

It is the shortest verse in the Bible, yet perhaps the most profound:
Jesus wept. Not because He lacked faith or was weak or afraid.
Not because He forgot resurrection was coming.
He wept because grief was present.

This moment was not staged or polite.
It was raw, vulnerable, and human.
And it tells you everything about how God feels about your emotions:
He is never afraid to enter them with you.

Tears have a language Heaven understands, saying what words cannot.
 They release what fear grips too tightly.
They remind you that you are human
 and that God loves you enough to feel the pain with you.

Tears are not a weakness; they are the body's way of releasing and healing.
Neuroscience teaches that tears carry cortisol and stress hormones,
helping your body discharge tension and regulate itself.

Yet many of us were taught that God wants our strength, not our softness.
Men are socialized to suppress tears.
We are conditioned to believe faith means smiling through suffering.

But Jesus did not hide His sorrow.
He wept, and still moved in power.
If Jesus could cry, then so can you.

Your emotions do not disqualify you from healing;
they are part of the process.
I have cried the kind of tears that can salt the soul,
after my sister's sudden passing,
through long nights of questioning,
and weary days of tears and more tears.

I learned that crying when sorrow has already spoken first
does begin the long healing process.
We do not have to apologize for our tears.
We ought to remember instead: Jesus wept too.
He did not rush through grief.
He stood in it.
He felt it.
He showed it.
He let the ache breathe,
and the world saw love move through His tears.
When we finally allow our own tears to fall,
we discover that God does not step back from us;
He draws us closer.

Whisper from God
"You don't have to hold them in.
I created the water that falls from your eyes, and I count every drop.
You're not falling apart; you are emptying what I am ready to heal.
Let the tears fall, My beloved. I'm right here, catching them all."
— Love, God

DR. PATRICIA SAYS...
"Tears are truth leaving the body, grief is an expression
of love and longing,
They don't make you fragile; they make you free.
Even in neuroscience, tears reset the brain's stress response.
And spiritually, they reset the soul."

DAY 16

When Shame Whispers

SCRIPTURE ANCHOR

"Therefore, there is now no condemnation for those who are in Christ Jesus."
—*Romans 8:1* (NIV)

Shame has a quiet voice.
It hides in our posture,
in polite smiles,
in our Happy Sabbaths,
in the way we avoid mirrors, people, and places.

Sometimes it whispers in the background of your thoughts:
"You should be over this by now."
"You are too emotional."
"You are failing at healing."
"God must be tired of you."

But shame lies.
And those lies create **Emotional Echoes™**,
where past wounds project themselves onto the present.
So even when God is offering you grace,
your nervous system may still brace for judgment.

That is what makes shame so heavy.
It hijacks your healing
and convinces you that the pain you carry is your fault.
But here is the truth:

God does not condemn you,
not for your tears,
not for your trauma,

not for the way your body, your mind, or your emotions
are healing slower than you hoped.

At sixteen, I learned to straighten my back against scoliosis,
while secretly wishing my spine could mirror my prayers:
upright, unbent, not merely acceptable but beautiful.
At eighteen, it was my gray hair I kept coloring.
Today, it is wiping the tears that arrive too quickly when grief returns.

The older I grew, the softer I became.
And in that softness, shame began to lose its sound.
Because God never turned His face from the curve, the gray, or the grief.
He called them evidence of endurance, not error,
and He gave them a healing voice in my ministry,
a place where my story could touch others,
offering comfort and confidence.

Healing is not a linear path; it is a holy one.
And there is no shame in needing time, safety, and grace.
When shame tries to tell you that you are too far gone,
let Romans 8:1 speak louder: No condemnation. Not now. Not ever.

Whisper from God
"I never asked you to hide what I can make holy.
The parts you think disqualify you are
the ones I use to draw others near.
Lift your head, my beloved.
You were never unworthy, only unfinished."
— Love, God

DR. PATRICIA SAYS...
"Ladies, our shame is learned in emotional survival,
but unlearned in love and acceptance.
Every time you show up as you are,
you tell your nervous system: I am still safe.
I am still seen, I am worthy, beautiful and royal."

DAY 17

Not Anxious. Anchored

SCRIPTURE ANCHOR

"You will keep in perfect peace those whose minds are steadfast, because they trust in You."
—Isaiah 26:3 (NKJV)

Some days, peace feels like a distant hope—
as though it is dangling on Mars, just out of reach.
You pray. You breathe. You journal.
You smile, brush your hair, put on your favorite pumps,
and still your thoughts begin to spiral.

But here is the truth:
anxiety does not disqualify you from peace.
It simply reveals where your nervous system is still learning that it is safe.
Peace is not a place without fear;
peace is the place where fear finds a Friend.

In trauma recovery, we speak about the difference between top-down and bottom-up healing.
Your mind might know you are safe,
but your body might still be reacting as though you are in danger.
That is not a spiritual failure; it is a biological one.

And yet, Isaiah 26:3 offers a gentle promise:
peace is not manufactured by control;
it is maintained through trust.
Not the loud, performative kind,
but the quiet, anchoring trust that says,
"Even if I feel flooded, I know Who holds me."

I remember my husband and I standing in the airport,
watching our teenage girls board flights to places I could not protect them:
Miami, Trinidad, El Salvador, Guatemala.
My mother-heart tried to look calm,
but inside, I rehearsed every what-if?

Tears flowed; it was raining on the inside and the outside.
I prayed hard and breathed shallow.
That is when God taught me something beautiful and biblical:
trust is not pretending you are unafraid.
It is admitting that you are, and still believing He is near.

My body calmed as I remembered what my soul already knew:
Ife, Elle-Michelle, and Prince were never just mine!
They were His first!
His eyes are on them,
and His Spirit is always near.

Whisper from God
"You don't have to grip the world to keep it safe.
I am already holding what you love.
Let go, not into the unknown, but into My arms."
— Love, God

DR. PATRICIA SAYS...
Anxiety is the body's alarm for love and safety.
But peace is God's way of answering it.
When you anchor your paced breathing to His presence,
your heart learns safety again."

DAY 18

The Voice That Calms the Spiral

SCRIPTURE ANCHOR

"Be still, and know that I am God"
—Psalm 46:10 (NKJV)

Stillness once made me nervous.
I could not just sit in quietude;
my mind was always wandering what else I could be doing.
It felt like a waste of time,
as if I was not doing enough to become who God made me to be,
to be the wife, mother, sister, and daughter who held the world together.

But the longer I live,
the more I realize stillness is not silence; it is surrender.

When your nervous system has been shaped by perfectionism, trauma, or chaos, movement can feel safer than stillness.
Stillness can feel like vulnerability, exposure, even danger.
Stillness can feel unsafe until Love redefines it.

God redefines stillness as a place of divine protection, not human pressure.
His voice does not compete with chaos;
it speaks through calm,
that still, small voice that assures the soul.

When I stopped filling every quiet space with projects and ministry,
I began to hear what peace actually sounds like.
It started early in the morning,
just as I woke,
before the clamor of responsibility filled my thoughts. I could hear His voice.

Now, when my mind begins to spiral into the six million things I have to do,
I whisper, Be still, Patricia,
and I imagine His hand resting gently on my shoulders,
steadying the rise and fall of my breath, ebbing away at the anxious thoughts.

This is where healing can begin:
where your body stops bracing,
where your thoughts stop racing,
where your soul begins to settle beneath His touch
and the sound of one voice:
The Voice of the One who never leaves.

Stillness is not something you force.
It is something you receive.

I am learning to be still, always remembering:
He has the whole world in His hands,
and He has mine as well.

Whisper from God
"You do not have to earn My peace, daughter.
Let your striving rest, and allow the purpose I created you for
to settle within you. The storm may keep speaking,
but My voice is stronger and more persistent.
Be still,
I am here."
— Love, God

DR. PATRICIA SAYS...
"Stillness is the nervous system's worship.
It tells the brain, I am safe now.
And in that safety, God's whisper becomes clear again."

DAY 19

You're Still in the Story

SCRIPTURE ANCHOR

"...being confident of this, that He who began a good work in you will carry it on to completion..."
— Philippians 1:6 (NIV)

I once worked in an environment that dimmed my light,
where kindness was mistaken for weakness,
and faithful competence was met with hostility.
I prayed for escape, but God was teaching endurance.

It took time to see it,
how the same pressure meant to break me
was actually fortifying my voice.
When He finally moved me to a new space,
I did not just walk out stronger;
I walked out softer.

Because healing is not just surviving the chapter,
it is trusting the Author who still writes your name with purpose.
Every wrinkle in your timeline strengthens your core.
Every scar tells your story.
El Roi sees, and He says,
"I will use it for your legacy."

Yet sometimes healing feels like failure.
You started strong, prayed the prayers,
did the work, and showed up with courage.
But then came the relapse, the numbness, the spiral, the shutdown.
And shame whispers, "See? You are still broken."

But here is the truth:
you are not at the end of your story,
you are in the middle of your healing.

Philippians 1:6 is not a motivational verse,
it is a divine, trauma-informed promise:
God does not abandon what He begins.
Your regression did not cancel His process.
He is faithful to finish what He started in you.

Even in therapy, we expect resistance and rupture
they are part of the transformation.
Your healing with God is no different.
There will be days when you grieve old versions of yourself,
days when you wonder if the work was worth it.
But those are the very days this verse stands taller than your fear:
He is not done.

This is the brilliance of divine authorship:
God knows how to write through trauma.
He includes your survival, your shutdowns, your silent seasons,
and still calls it good work in progress.

You do not need a perfect ending
to be living in a holy process.

Whisper from God
"They didn't end your story; they advanced it.
I turn closed doors into corridors of destiny.
Keep walking, beloved, I'm not done writing."
— Love, God

DR. PATRICIA SAYS...
"Every hard place has a curriculum.
What felt like exile was actually editing.
You're not lost in the plot, you're being refined in the process, you are
the protagonist."

DAY 20

When Healing Looks Like Release

SCRIPTURE ANCHOR

"He restores my soul."
— Psalm 23:3 (NKJV)

You thought healing would feel like fireworks,
like instant deliverance, like a big, bold breakthrough.

But instead, it feels quieter than you imagined.
Because healing often looks like release, not arrival,
like discovering your core values and saying "no" without apologizing,
like crying in front of someone and not rushing to explain it,
like feeling your feelings and not flinching from the release.

Healing does not always feel beautiful or holy.
Sometimes it feels like quiet dignity,
like walking away when provoked or ill-treated,
like blessing those who misunderstood you,
like choosing peace over proof.
Like forgiving even when wounds are still healing.

Psalm 23 does not say, He fixes my life.
It says, He restores my *soul*.

And restoration is subtle. It is nervous-system work.
It is spiritual reparenting.
It is letting the Emotional Echo™ of fear fade as truth grows louder.
It is having one tender moment where your first instinct is not self-blame or self-protection.

You may not realize you are healing until you are already in the middle of it.
Suddenly, the anger softens. The spiral slows.
The silence feels safe instead of scary.

You begin to recognize God,
not just in your victories,
but in your regulated breath,
your sacred "no,"
your peaceful pause.
You are not faking it anymore.
You are healing,
and it is working.

There came a day when I realized
I no longer needed to explain my God-given light
to those who feared its shine.
That was the moment I knew restoration had taken root.
Hallelujah! Praise the Lord who gave it to me!

Now, when others act from their **Emotional Echo™**,
I see pain, not the person.
And that perspective
is mercy,
it is the mark of a healing soul.

Whisper from God
"You're free now, My beloved.
Free to bless others and let their hate, discouragement, and disregard
go. Free to see their wound without reopening yours.
This is restoration, my beloved daughter, it's quiet, sacred, complete."
— Love, God

DR. PATRICIA SAYS...
"Healing is when you can stay kind in the face of cruelty.
When peace becomes your reflex, not your reward.
That's how you know your soul has been restored."

DAY 21

It's Okay to Say You're Not Okay

SCRIPTURE ANCHOR

"How long, Lord? Will you forget me forever?
How long will you hide your face from me?"
— Psalm 31:1 (NIV)

Some days you feel like you should be further along.
Should be "over it" by now.
Should have more faith.
Should not be triggered anymore.
Should not still cry about what happened.
But all those "shoulds" are shame in disguise.
And shame has no place in healing.

Psalm 13 shows us something radical:
You can be a person of faith and still feel forgotten, lost.
You can love God deeply and still ask:
"Where are You, Lord?" And He doesn't flinch when you do.

This is the emotional permission we've been missing in spiritual spaces,
like at home, in church, or with friends.
Hey queens, can we PLEASE create safe spaces for Emotional Disrobing™
The freedom to say:
"I'm not okay right now."
"I don't feel strong."
"I love God, but I'm tired of the silence."

David, the man after God's own heart, wrote these words from the valley,
not the mountaintop. And God included them in Scripture.
That is proof that your unfiltered feelings do not disqualify you.
In fact, they might be the very doorway to deeper intimacy with God,
and with yourself.

When my mother passed away, it felt as if the whole world tilted...it no longer existed as God intended. Something deep inside me shattered in a place no one else could see, a silent wound that throbbed with every breath. When asked about her passing, I caught myself retelling the story so often that it began to sound rehearsed, as though I had managed the pain. But inside that deep space, I was still aching badly. So, I resolved to start telling the truth: "I am not okay. I am hurting. My soul has collapse under a weight I didn't think my heart could carry. My mom's absence tore through me with a grief that had no edges and no end. Yes, I am in this pain even when I show up in the world. I feel motherless. I am left without her prayers, her wisdom, and her steadying presence!"

So, it is okay to name your ache.
God will not walk away.
He will lean in closer.

Whisper from God
"I'm not offended by your pain.
I'm not disappointed by your doubt.
I'm not ashamed of your sadness.
I'd rather have your honesty than your silence.
Don't clean it up for Me.
I already see it. Just let Me hold it with you.
You don't have to be okay
to be close."
— Love, God

DR. PATRICIA SAYS...
"Permission to feel is the beginning of permission to heal.
Emotional Disrobing™ means you stop hiding your hurt—
and let your vulnerability become sacred.
You're not falling apart.
You're finally being honest
and real"

WEEK 4: Anchored in Surrender

SCRIPTURE ANCHOR

"Trust in the Lord with all your heart and lean not on your own understanding."

—Proverbs 5:3(NIV)

To heal is to surrender. Not as defeat, but as deliverance.
Faith is not loudest when the fig tree blooms,
it is loudest when you worship in the barrenness of life,
when you reach for God while you are still bleeding,
when you lean into Him while trembling with fear.
This week is all about unclenching your fists.
About realizing that trust does not have to roar, sometimes it whispers.
You will learn that faith is not pretending you are okay;
it is daring to reach when you are not.
That worship is not noise; it is presence.
That surrender is not losing control;
it is resting in the hands of the One who has always held you.
By the end of this week, you will discover
that surrender is not weakness.
It is the safest strength you will ever know.

DAY 22

The Hardest Place to Worship From

SCRIPTURE ANCHOR

"Though the fig tree does not bud and there are no grapes on the vines... yet I will rejoice in the Lord, I will be joyful in God my Savior."
— Habakkuk 3:17–18 (NIV)

Worship is easy when life is blooming.
When the school fees and mortgage are paid.
When the body is beautiful and healed.
When the prayers are answered and your heart feels light.

But what about when the fig tree doesn't bud?
When a loved one walked away or a treasured relationship ends.
When the diagnosis drops and the heart weighs heavy.
When the prayers seem to hit the ceiling and bounce right back unanswered.

Habakkuk did not worship because things got better.
No he did not! He worshiped while it still hurt.
While the vines were still bare, fruitless.
While his hope was still trembling, he worshiped
That's what made it beautiful and holy.

I saw that kind of worship in my mother.
She sang hymns and prayed when times were difficult,
when her body was wearied by earthly labors
but not from hours of prayer,
when uncertainty threatened, but could not steal her peace.
She worshiped from a place knowing that He was present.

Worship while in difficult spaces isn't denial.
It's not pretending.
It's choosing intimacy with God over explanation.
It's whispering, "Even if nothing changes,
I'll still meet You here."

You don't have to lift your voice loudly for it to count.
Sometimes worship is a whisper.
Sometimes it's tears on your pillow.
Sometimes it's just not giving up, even when the odds seem sealed and stacked against you.

And sometimes worship is simply breathing in the awareness of His presence, even when you feel too tired to pray.

It is choosing stillness over striving, letting your trembling heart lean into the One who has never once trembled about you. This, too, is worship, and Heaven receives it.

This kind of worship rewires the nervous system by teaching your body what your soul already knows. You are safe, even in sorrow. You are held, even in the hollow places.

Whisper from God
"I see the cost of your praise.
I know it's not easy to lift your head right now.
But you don't have to fake joy — I'm not looking for performance.
I'm looking for presence.
Your worship — wounded and weary — is still welcome.
I count every tear as holy.
Keep coming. I'm here."
— Love, God

DR. PATRICIA SAYS...
"Worship while hurting is trauma-integrated faith.
It's when the survival brain softens enough to say:
'I'm not okay... but I'm not alone.'
That's not weakness — that's spiritual resilience.
And that resilience is how healing begins."

DAY 23

Faith While You're Still Bleeding

SCRIPTURE ANCHOR

"If I can just touch His robe, I will be healed"
— Matthew 9:21 (NLT)

She didn't come to Jesus clean and polished.
She came bleeding.
Twelve years of disappointment and rejection,
twelve years of being labeled unclean,
twelve years of trying everything and everyone, but only getting worse.

But still… she reached.
She reached in faith.

She existed on the fringe of society.
She wasn't supposed to be in that crowd.
Her bleeding made her untouchable,
but her faith made her healing possible.
And what she didn't know was that Jesus wasn't just a healer;
He was a safe place for shame to break.

When she touched Him, power flowed.
But when He turned to her, His presence flowed.
He called her "Daughter", not issue, not condition, not unclean.
His words restored more than her body;
they redefined her identity.
She was unclean, untouchable… but still His.

I, too have had seasons of bleeding,
not always visible, but deeply felt.
Even when my lips could not form words to describe
being overlooked, being judged, and being denied opportunities
all hidden behind a strong, determined face.

And like her, I have reached for Jesus in faith and heartfelt prayers.
I have held on to His promises and the belief
that He has a magnificent plan for my life.
And every single time, He didn't turn away, He turned toward me.

That's what faith while bleeding does.
It doesn't wait for perfection.
It reaches for God in the middle of the hurt,
the discomfort and the messiness.
Because the miracle is not just in being healed, it's in being seen.
You may still be bleeding, still waiting and wanting,
still hurting and hoping. But your reach still counts.
And Jesus still turns toward you.

Whisper from God
"I saw you reach.
I felt the faith in your trembling hand.
Your bleeding does not put me off,
I'm moved by it.
I don't just want to heal your issue,
I want to name you:
Precious Daughter.
Beloved.
Mine.
I know what it cost you to come close.
I honor your reach."
— Love, God

DR. PATRICIA SAYS...
"Faith, while bleeding, is a sacred nervous system act.
When trauma tells you to shut down, but your spirit still reaches,
that's healing in motion.
That's Emotional Disrobing™.
And that's when Jesus doesn't just heal you —
He sees you."

DAY 24

Held in the Breaking

SCRIPTURE ANCHOR

"He heals the brokenhearted and binds up their wounds."
— Psalm 147:3 (NIV)

Breaking rarely ever looks pretty or holy.
Sometimes it looks like tears you can not explain,
or silence that feels too heavy to hold.
Sometimes it is sitting at the kitchen table,
wondering how to keep being strong for everyone else
when you are not sure how to hold yourself together.

I have known that kind of breaking.
When my mother passed at ninety-two,
grief came in waves: soft, then sudden.
It was the kind that both emptied my soul and anchored me.
And even in that hollow awful ache,
I found that God was still holding what I could not.
He was holding my purpose safe and secure
That is when Restore Your Royalty was born,
out of the cracks, not the crowns, came a program for healing women.

In clinical work, we call this the release point,
when the body finally exhales what the soul has carried too long.
It is not a weakness.
It is wisdom.
Your nervous system knows when it is safe enough to let go.

And God never flinches at that moment.
He does not rush the tears.
He allows them to flow at a safe pace for your healing
He does not bring shame or blame
He binds wounds, not with quick fixes,

but with his gentle, powerful presence, patient, quiet, and steady.

You don't have to hurry through the breaking.
You don't have to explain it.
You have to let Him hold you
until your breath steadies again.
That's where your restoration begins,
right in the middle of what is still trembling.

Whisper from God
"I am not asking you to be strong.
I will always be here, even when you are broken,
holding the pieces others cannot see.
You do not have to hide your breaking from Me.
Every fragment of you matters.
Every piece still belongs.
Let Me be the hands that hold
what is holy in the shattered places.
Let your heart know:
Your restoration has begun."
— Love, God

DR. PATRICIA SAYS...
"The breaking is not your undoing; it is your unveiling.
When the body finally trusts Presence enough to release,
healing begins to move through the broken places.
God does not rush repair.
He restores through His Presence,
and in that slow restoration,
wholeness becomes your worship."

DAY 25

When Trust Is a Tremble, Not a Roar

SCRIPTURE ANCHOR

"Trust in the Lord with all your heart and lean not on your own understanding. In all your ways acknowledge him and He will make your paths straight."
— Proverbs 3:5 (NIV)

Trusting is not always understanding God's plan.
It is acknowledging His Lordship,
and sometimes it sounds like a whisper:
"Okay, God… I'll try again even if I cannot see the path."

Sometimes it looks like showing up when your heart is still bruised.
Sometimes it is simply not walking away, even when confused and unsure.
Sometimes it is choosing stillness when everything in you wants to run.

It is taking one gentle breath in God's direction,
letting your trembling faith be enough for today.
It is belief that He holds the map
even when all you can see is the very next small step.

I have known that tremble:
stepping out, not knowing where to put the next foot,
holding on to quiet faith that shows up even when I can't see the outcome.
Like the season, I faced uncertainty at work and in leadership,
still choosing to show up, voice shaking, but spirit willing.

We were taught that trust is confidence,
but trauma teaches us that to trust is to take a risk.
It is handing over what hurt you before.
It is leaning into the unknown again and again,
because He is known to you.

Here is what God never does:
He never shames your fear or your tremble.
He never demands boldness you don't have.
He says, "Trust."
Not on your logic.
Not on your perfectionism or people-pleasing.
Not on your ability, nor on your strength. Just trust in Me.

Trust because I am already in tomorrow,
making straight what feels crooked to you today.

So it is these moments of fear where trust is built,
moments when you choose not to run.
Not because you understand,
but because you are starting to believe
that God is safe and capable of directing your path.

And even when your hands shake while reaching,
He still calls it trust. And He can still make your paths straight.

Whisper from God
"I see how hard it is to trust again.
I will not rush you. I will not force you.
I will stand beside you as you lean a little at a time.
And when your trust feels like a whisper,
I still hear it like a song.
You don't need roaring faith, only a heart willing to reach."
— Love, God

DR. PATRICIA SAYS...
"Trauma reshapes trust—it teaches the body that trusting is dangerous.
But healing teaches you how to trust again, slowly and authentically.
Trembling trust is still trust, and God honors it.
He sees you."

DAY 26

He Sees the Trauma You Don't Speak

SCRIPTURE ANCHOR

"You are the God who sees me."
— Genesis 16:13 *(NIV)*

Hagar wasn't asking to be noticed.
She was running.
Pregnant. Rejected. Misunderstood.
She had every reason to believe her pain didn't matter,
She was just a servant. Just a surrogate. Just a problem.
That she was too small, too insignificant for heaven to see.

But in the wilderness, God came looking for her.
Not to correct her. Not to shame her. But to see her.

And when He did, she named Him
El Roi : "The God who sees me."

There are moments in my own story that echo hers.
Times I have smiled through a room full of people and still felt invisible.
Times I have held grief in my chest until it hummed like a secret.
Times I have shown up strong because I did not have words for the weariness underneath.

There are parts of you, too, that no one has seen.
Not the tears in the shower.
Not the quiet panic in a crowded room.
Not the ache that lingers long after the event has passed.

But God saw it.
He saw the tremor behind the composure.
He saw the long exhale after holding it all together.
And instead of asking for explanations,

He offered his comforting presence.
God sees trauma differently than people do.
He sees the imprint it leaves on your nervous system, how you flinch when touched, how you scan for shifts in someone's voice,
how you over-function to avoid abandonment.

Here is God's truth: You don't have to name every trauma to be healed.
You don't have to explain your nervous system's reactions to be understood.
When He sees you, it is not just looking at you; it is His compassion.
You don't need to speak it for God to start binding it.

The One who knitted you together has never missed a moment of you.
He sees the flash in your eyes when old memories rise.
He sees how your body tightens at a tone that sounds too familiar.
He sees the ache that language cannot explain
And still...He stays.

Whisper from God
"I saw what they didn't.
I know the story behind your silence.
You don't need to translate your tears for Me.
I was there for the breaking,
and I am here for the rebuilding.
I just wanted to let you know that nothing about you is unseen.
Nothing about you is too much.
I see, and I stay."
— Love, God

DR. PATRICIA SAYS...
"The nervous system remembers what words forget.
But safety begins when you realize you are seen,
not for performance,
but for presence.
Being seen by God is the beginning of being soothed.
And that's where real healing begins."

DAY 27

What Happens When You Don't Feel Spiritual

SCRIPTURE ANCHOR

"In the same way, the Spirit helps us in our weakness. We do not know what we ought to pray for, but the Spirit himself intercedes for us through wordless groans."
— Romans 8:26 *(NIV)*

There are mornings when your Bible stays closed
and your heart feels miles away from worship.
When prayer sounds like static.
When even the language of faith feels foreign on your tongue.
I've known those mornings.
When grief made me stare at the ceiling and whisper,
"God, I don't even have words today."

But here's what Romans 8 reminds us, silence is not failure;
The Spirit becomes translator for the things too deep to say.
When your breath shakes, He turns it into prayer.
When tears fall, He gathers them like language.
When exhaustion replaces eloquence, He intercedes.

This is grace for the nervous system:
When you are emotionally depleted, mentally foggy, or physically weary,
you don't have to perform your faith.
God is still moving.

Your energy level doesn't measure your spirituality.
His unrelenting presence measures it.

Healing means learning that even in your quietest, weakest moments,
you're not less loved.
You're not less chosen.
You're not less seen.

Sometimes, the deepest worship is simply being still enough for the Spirit to translate what you can't say
This is what grace looks like for the nervous system:
When your mind can't focus and your body feels heavy, heaven does not withdraw.
You don't lose your spirituality when you lose your strength.
God moves toward you in the quiet you.

I have learned that holiness sometimes hides in the smallest gestures:
a sigh instead of a lengthy, flowery sermon,
a breath instead of a battle cry of an army,
a moment of stillness instead of striving for endless movement.
You are still His, even when your faith feels wordless.

Whisper from God
"Beloved, I'm not waiting for perfect prayers.
I already understand the groans beneath your silence.
I see your fatigue, your blank pages, your unspoken ache.
You don't have to push through the weariness to reach Me.
I'm already here—closer than your next breath.
Even when you don't feel spiritual, you are still Mine."
— Love, God

DR. PATRICIA SAYS…
"When your nervous system is overwhelmed, quiet becomes holy.
Tears become prayer.
Presence becomes worship.
Healing isn't about performance; it's about permission.
Even when you can't find words for God,
grace is fluent in your silence."

DAY 28

You Are Not a Burden, You Belong

SCRIPTURE ANCHOR

"But now in Christ Jesus you who once were far away have been brought near by the blood of Christ."
— Ephesians 2:13 *(NIV)*

Some wounds do not just hurt—they isolate.
You start to believe things like:
"My needs are a burden."
"If I let them in they will hurt me."
"If I slow down, everything will fall apart."
"I should be over this by now."
"I have to earn love."
 "No one would understand."

But here is what trauma gets wrong:
it confuses being hurt with being unworthy, and you will never be unworthy

That is the **emotional echo** that reverberates through the nervous system,
telling you that your pain makes you a burden,
that your story takes up too much space.
So you begin responding to the present through the pain of the past.

But the gospel breaks that echo into splinterings with this truth:
You are not too broken for belonging.
You are not too complicated.
Not too messy.
Not too late.
Not too far.
Glory, my sisters! What great news this is for our hearts and minds!

Ephesians 2:13 says you have been brought near,
not by performance,

not by perfection,
not by your healing milestones,
but by the blood of Christ.
You do not earn belonging.
It is your divine lineage.

And God does not simply tolerate you in His presence.
He welcomes you.
He wants you close,
even when you are unraveling,
even when you are uncertain,
even when you are not yet "fixed."

I want you to know that your story is welcome. Your trauma is safe. Your heart still has a home with God.

Whisper from God
"You belong here.
Not when you have healed.
Not when you are less emotional.
Not when you have figured it out.
Now. As you are.
I am the God who draws near, not away.
You have never been too broken for Me.
I have made room for your whole story—
especially the parts others tried to erase."
— Love, God

DR. PATRICIA SAYS...
"Rejection creates a nervous system that scans for disconnection.
But healing rewires that scan to receive safety.
You do not heal to belong—you heal in belonging.
God makes space for your full humanity—and still calls you His"

WEEK 5: Anchored in Strength

SCRIPTURE ANCHOR

"But those who hope in the Lord will renew their strength. They will soar on wings like eagles; they will run and not grow weary, they will walk and not be faint."

—Isaiah 40:31(NIV)

Strength is not the absence of struggle: it is the presence of resilience. And resilience is born when your scars stop speaking shame and start speaking story.

This week is about reclaiming your power and realizing that you are not what you have been through. You are who God says you are: chosen, royal, and wonderfully made. Strength doesn't mean you never feel fragile. It means you rise in the middle of fragility, wearing your crown while remembering the dust you came from.

And somewhere in that rising, forgiveness begins to bloom. It is not permission for what hurt you. It is a release from what no longer serves you. Forgiveness is how peace takes root. It is the quiet proof that your healing has become holy.

By the end of this week, you will not only feel stronger, but also more confident. You will know your strength comes from being rooted, released, and redeemed.

DAY 29

You Are Not What You've Been Through

SCRIPTURE ANCHOR

"Therefore, if anyone is in Christ, the new creation has come: The old has gone, the new is here!"
— 2 Corinthians 5:17 (NIV)

Your story may include trauma, but trauma is not your identity. Still, it lingers: in how you speak, in how you love, in how quickly you brace for disappointment.

When the pain stays too long, it tries to rename you:
Difficult.
Damaged.
Too much.
Not enough.
Too needy.
And sometimes you actually embrace those lies.
You may not say it, but it seeps out in the
boundaries you're afraid to set,
the apologies you whisper for simply existing,
the way you shrink so others feel comfortable,
Or the way you wear armor so they never notice your pain.

But God never asks your wounds to write your name.
He does not consult your critics or your past to define your worth.
He calls you new. Not because you escaped the fire,
but because you are no longer owned by it.

You have been refined by it.
I have known what it feels like to be misunderstood,
to have supervisors whose envy turned to quiet sabotage,
to see doors close that God Himself had opened.
Yet, even there, He whispered, "Forgive."

Not because they were right, but because I needed to be restored.
Forgiveness became my act of resistance.
It was my refusal to let bitterness write my story.
It was choosing freedom instead of replaying the wound.
It was letting God hold the justice so my heart could finally rest.

That is what healing does. It does not erase your history. It rewrites your identity. And that rewriting happens deep within your nervous system. Where fear once ruled, peace begins to settle and reign. Where you once flinched, you now breathe.

Where you once expected abandonment, you now prepare for connection. Where you once over-performed to be seen, you now rest, knowing you already are. You have been through fire, but fire did not name you. God did!

Whisper from God
"I saw the moments they tried to limit you.
I saw the pain of being overlooked, the silence you held instead of striking back.
I have not forgotten the tears you cried in faith.
You are not your rejection, beloved.
You are My reflection.
I am still restoring what others tried to reduce.
You are Mine—whole, healed, and becoming new."
— Love, God

DR. PATRICIA SAYS...
"Forgiveness does not excuse injustice,
it evicts it from your nervous system.
When envy or betrayal meet grace, healing takes the throne.
You are not what you have been through;
you are what survived, surrendered,
and you still chose love."

DAY 30

He Calls You His Own

SCRIPTURE ANCHOR

"Do not fear, for I have redeemed you; I have called you by name; you are Mine."
— Isaiah 43:1 (NIV)

When I was six, my parents separated.
My father's absence became its own kind of presence:
it was there in the quiet of our home,
at birthdays, Father's Day, and Christmas,
in the unspoken ache that lingered in my heart. Until it went into hiding.

But my mother, a quintessential God-fearing woman,
anchored me in a different truth:
your identity goes beyond genes; it reaches all the way to heaven.
She taught me that even when people walk away, God stays.

There is a kind of healing that happens when someone says your name and means it. Not because you are convenient. Not because you are performing. But because you belong.

God does not just save you. He names you. He claims you and says, "You are Mine."
It is not ownership. It is affection.
It is not controlled. It is a covenant.
It is not possession. It is protection.
It is identity-rooted love.

For those of us who have known rejection, those words land like oxygen.
Because when abandonment writes its script on the nervous system,
your body learns to brace for goodbye even in safe places.
But God interrupts that loop with a phrase that changes everything:
"You. Are. Mine."

Even when you are questioning.
Even when you are not healed yet.
Even when you do not feel spiritual.
Even when you are doubting or unraveling.
Even when you still ache for the father, the friend,
or the figure who walked away and did not look back.

Even then, He calls you by name:
not by your wounds, not by your issues,
not by your weakness, not by your worthiness,
not by your mistakes, not by your roles,
but by your name.

And then He speaks belonging over you again and again:
"You are Mine." Not in part. Not if. Not someday. Now. Entirely. Forever!
He has promised, "…I will never leave thee, nor forsake thee." Hebrews 13:5

Whisper from God
"I saw you when the chair was empty and the questions were loud.
I've been your Father in the shadows and your covering in the storm.
I have never confused you with your pain.
I have always called you by name.
You are Mine — not borrowed, not broken, not forgotten.
You are home."
— Love, God

DR. PATRICIA SAYS...
"The echoes of absence can live deep in the nervous system, but divine love speaks louder.
You are not the sum of who didn't stay; you are the story of Who always does.
When God calls you 'Mine,' belonging becomes your birthright and forgiveness, even toward unmet needs, becomes freedom."

DAY 31

Chosen with a Purpose

SCRIPTURE ANCHOR

"For he chose us in him before the creation of the world to be holy and blameless in his sight. In love""
— Ephesians 1:4 *(NIV)*

My mother never wore a crown, but she lived like royalty: steady, prayerful, and anchored in grace.
Her strength wasn't loud, but it was luminous.
Watching her choose faith in every season planted a profound truth in me.
Royalty isn't about power. It is about a chosen posture.

She chose and carried that same royal posture into her work as a principal, lifting families who were struggling
and standing as a steadying pillar in our community.
She led with compassion rather than control, and her presence became a refuge long before I understood the word 'ministry'.
She was leadership wrapped in love.
Watching her serve taught me what divine authority really looks like.

Years later, in the lecture hall, in the clinician's chair, and in the places where the pain of others met my purpose, I saw that same quiet strength rise again.
This time, it was in me.
Grief over her passing did not end my story.
It birthed Restore Your Royalty, a movement reminding women who they already are: royal, beloved, anointed, chosen.

Being chosen is not about perfection. It is about alignment.
God doesn't need polished vessels. He needs willing ones. He chooses us through the breaking, not after it.

He turns wounds into wisdom, classrooms into sanctuaries,
and ordinary work into holy purpose that serves others.
You are royal not because you have never bent,
but because you rise again and carry grace like your crown.
Your purpose was never lost.
It was simply waiting for your acceptance and your "yes."

You are God's special possession. Not a possession to control.
Instead, the one He protects, restores, and sends with purpose.
Living your purpose does not begin when you become perfect.
It begins when you say, "Yes... even from where I am right now."

Trauma may have tried to reduce you to roles of pleasing, protecting, and performing, but healing helps you rise as royalty: grounded, called, and commissioned for His greatness. You are not just recovering. You are reclaiming what was always divinely yours.

Whisper from God
"I chose you, knowing every season you would walk through.
I saw the grief, the growth, the grit, and I still said yes.
You are My royal daughter, called to carry light into weary places.
I'm not waiting for you to be perfect; I'm inviting you to be present.
Rise, beloved, your purpose is already unfolding."
— Love, God

DR. PATRICIA SAYS...
"Legacy and calling are woven together. My mother modeled prayer;
my purpose became restoration.
Healing taught me that chosen-ness isn't a title: it's a trust.
You don't have to chase significance; you carry it.
When you say yes to your calling, heaven amplifies your voice."

DAY 32

There's a Gift in Your Sensitivity

"I praise You because I am fearfully and wonderfully made; Your works are wonderful, I know that full well."
— Psalm 139:14 (NIV)

When I was a child, my mother would smile and say,
"Patricia, you think too deeply."
She was right. I noticed everything:
the sighs behind smiles,
the quiet sadness in someone's eyes,
the child sitting alone,
the senior church member everyone overlooked.

As a teenager, that awareness became action.
I could not walk past the downtrodden without wanting to help.
What I did not know was that empathy
was already written into my nervous system.
Sensitivity was woven into the way my brain and heart connect,
propelling me to notice, to nurture, to care.

God built me to feel deeply, to notice gently, and to care fully.
For years, I wondered why others moved on quickly while I lingered in reflection, but now I see it:
My empathy is not excessive; it is evidence of God's craftsmanship.

It was not something to fix,
but rather something that should be honored.
God's designs are on purpose.
Not as a flaw. Not as a weakness... But as capacity.

Life experience can heighten sensitivity,
but healing sanctifies it.
It transforms raw emotion into compassionate discernment.
It teaches you to care without carrying it all.
That is not fragility, that is spiritual intelligence.

Your empathy is a divine instrument. It is tuned to detect pain and offer peace, to hear need and answer with presence.
God made you that way on purpose.
Do not apologize for the depth that reflects His heart.

Yes, your experiences may have made your senses more alert, but God's healing teaches you how to live with sensitivity. Not in fear, but in His freedom. Where you once absorbed everything to survive, you can now feel deeply and remain sincere in serving others. This is what we call transformation.

This is where Emotional Echo™ shifts from reaction to discernment.
You begin to know what is yours to carry, and what is not.
You become emotionally wise without being overwhelmed.
You become empathic, but not enmeshed.
Your sensitivity is not a mistake.
It is part of your anointing, and that is DIVINE.

Whisper from God
"*I created your depth intentionally.*
You feel deeply because you love like Me.
Don't call it "too much."
It's how I designed you to heal, comfort, and connect.
Your tenderness is not weakness, it's worship."
— Love, God

Dr. Patricia Says...
"*Empathy is heavenly wiring*
the nervous system's way of mirroring the compassion of Christ.
When you stop seeing sensitivity as a flaw and start honoring it as a purpose,
your caring becomes strength.
You were never made to shut down.
You were made to show up with heart."

DAY 33

Loving Without Losing Yourself

"Above all else, guard your heart, for everything you do flows from it."
— Proverbs 4:23 (NIV)

For much of my life,
I believed loving well meant giving completely:
my time, my energy, my heart. I saw it in my mom, and it became me.

I poured myself into
my husband
my children
my work, and
my ministry, believing that level of sacrifice measured true love.

Yet, somewhere along the way,
I began to feel the quiet ache of disappearing inside the roles I carried.
The woman who loved deeply also needed space to breathe,
to hear her own thoughts about what her heart needed, and to reconnect
with the God who made her before she was anyone's
wife,
mother,
professor,
leader, or business owner.

Healing taught me that love is not measured by depletion.
It is measured by presence.
Being fully there for my family
did not mean losing the "me" God called by name.

The best gift I could give my children, my husband, my work, and my
ministry was a grounded, joyful, spiritually anchored version of myself.

So I had to create space where I could remain whole,
where silence restored me…

True love doesn't require self-erasure.
You can open your heart without abandoning yourself.
You don't have to disappear to prove your goodness.
This is emotional maturity rooted in grace.

When you learn to love from that center, that core, you don't run on empty.
You serve from overflow.
You love without losing yourself, you give without disappearing,
and you show up whole instead of drained.

From that anchored place, your "yes" is pure,
your compassion is sustainable, and your presence carries
a quiet strength that nourishes everyone connected to you.

And that overflow becomes the beautiful, steady, life-giving expression of love God always intended.
It is a love rooted in Him, not exhaustion.
A love that reflects wholeness, not depletion.
A love strong enough to lift others.
A love that first allowed God to lift you.

Whisper from God
"My daughter, I see how much you give.
Your devotion is beautiful to Me.
But I also delight in the quiet moments when you come apart to rest—
when you let Me refill what love has poured out.
You don't have to vanish to prove your value.
Abide in Me, and your love will never run dry."
— Love, God

DR. PATRICIA SAYS...
*"Presence is the purest form of love.
When you remain connected to who you are in God,
your giving becomes grace, not exhaustion.
The anchored heart loves deeply without losing itself."*

DAY 34

You Are Not Behind

"I will restore to you the years that the swarming locust has eaten..."
— Joel 42:25(ESV)

Over the past six years, I have experienced what I call a divine download: an outpouring of ideas, programs, and vision that came faster than I could execute. I filled pages with possibilities and prayed, "Lord, which one first?"
Then I would glance at my lists between family duties, home life, and ministry work...and feel the sting of falling behind.

Why did these ideas come now, when my hands already feel so full? Why not earlier, when life seemed freer? But he whispered, "Because this version of you is now ready to share this gift."

God reminded me that timing is never a punishment; it is a partnership... a divine collaboration between God and me.
He has purposed my life, and He knew exactly when I would be ready.

So the ideas did not come too late,
they came matured, ready to meet the version of me
who could carry them with wisdom, not striving.
The years behind me were not wasted;
they were shaping the knowledge and capacity needed
for this moment of divine alignment.

Out of that alignment, God birthed a series of faith-led, neuroscience-based, heart-healing programs: PACERS Parenting™, Couples Clinic HQ™, Heart & Mind Connection™, Restore Your Royalty™, and the Healthy Mentality Network™.

Each one is a reflection of God,
designed to help others experience what I have lived:
that healing can be holy,

and transformation can be both scientific and spiritual.
So if you are staring at your own list of dreams
and wondering when they will materialize, remember this truth:
You are not behind.
You are right on time for what Heaven has aligned.

And yes, discouragement will come,
sometimes from your own weary thoughts,
and sometimes from the voices around you
who cannot see what God is cultivating within you.
But do not let internal doubt or external noise
convince you that your calling is delayed or diminished.
Heaven's timeline is still intact,
and God's voice is louder than their disbelief
and kinder than your self-criticism.

Whisper from God
"Beloved, I gave you those visions because I trust you to nurture them, not rush them.
Your timing is My craftsmanship.
Nothing in your story is delayed—it's being developed.
Keep tending what's in your hands; I am cultivating what's in your heart.
You are not late, you're in rhythm with Me."
— Love, God

DR. PATRICIA SAYS...
*"The nervous system works in rhythm, not in a hurry.
When divine ideas come faster than your capacity,
it's not a race, it's revelation unfolding at heaven's pace.
You're not behind; you're being aligned."*

DAY 35

The Voice That Calls You Royal

"But you are a chosen people, a royal priesthood, a holy nation, God's special possession, that you may declare the praises of Him who called you out of darkness into His wonderful light."
— 1 Peter 2:9 (NIV)

I have always known that my life belonged to God.
Even when I was uncertain about my purpose, I was aware that He was present, steady, and guiding.
As the years unfolded, I began to discern His voice differently,
not calling me to do more,
but calling me to be more grounded in who I already was,
more confident in what He wanted to do in my life and through my life.

Royalty, I have learned, is not about reaching upward socially,
It's about becoming more deeply rooted in His truth.
It is acknowledging and finally believing the identity He has spoken over me.
It is the calm assurance that I am both crowned and covered,
not because I strive, but because I belong.
No performance is required for this identity;
only the steady acceptance of a divine inheritance I already carry.

And as that truth settles within you, something beautiful unfolds,
You begin to see royalty in others, too.
You recognize the divine inheritance they carry,
even when life has tried to tarnish their crown.
To walk in true royalty is not to elevate yourself above others,
but to celebrate the sacred dignity God has woven into every person.
When you honor the royalty in others, you multiply grace wherever you go.
You become a mirror of heaven's order,
where every son and daughter walks clothed in purpose,
crowned with compassion,
anchored in belonging.

And when a sister's crown tilts under the weight of life, you do not criticize;
you reach out in love and help her straighten it,
reminding her of who she already is...chosen, royal, and dearly loved.

Being royal means moving through the world with quiet authority.
With grace that listens before it speaks, stands firm before it reacts,
and leads with love rather than judgment or noise.
It is a stability born from knowing this: God's presence is my assurance.

As I grew spiritually, I came to understand more clearly that royalty isn't loud or lofty. No, it is peaceful, patient, and present.
It is the posture of a woman seated securely in her worth,
unhurried, unshaken, and unashamed of her calling...
confident in her core values and her boundaries. She can celebrate others and know that God's presence in her life makes her salt and light.

Whisper from God

*"Daughter of grace, I called you royal long before you believed it.
Your worth was sealed by My voice, not earned by your victories.
I placed a crown upon you, one that cannot be tarnished by rejection or removed by fear.
You do not need to strive to shine; you only need to remember whose light you carry. Lift your head, beloved. You wear My name.
You walk in My authority.
And wherever you go, heaven recognizes your crown."
— Love, God*

DR. PATRICIA SAYS...

*Royal identity begins in the brain long before it becomes visible in behavior. It is not about recovery.
It is about recognizing that you are already royalty.
When your nervous system learns that peace is power, your posture stops performing and starts standing in purpose.
This is the neuroscience of royalty.
It is where safety becomes serenity and serenity becomes strength.
You no longer strive to prove your worth. You embody it with grace.
This is anchored royalty: calm, centered, and confident in divine assignment.*

WEEK 6: Anchored in Mission

SCRIPTURE ANCHOR

"You crown the year with Your goodness, and Your paths drip with abundance."

—Psalm 65:11(NKJV)

Healing was never meant to end with you. It was meant to flow through you. This final week is about becoming the evidence of what grace can do, not by striving, but by abiding. Because when the heart is anchored and the nervous system learns safety, the soul begins to rise with purpose. You'll discover that your story was never just about recovery; it was about revelation.

The very places you once wept now hold wisdom.

The lessons you learned in the quiet now prepare you to lead with compassion. As a clinician and a woman of faith, I have come to see that healing and mission share the same root. Both are acts of surrender. God heals you to prepare you, not for performance, but for participation in His ongoing work of restoration. He invites you to build from wholeness. He invites you to lead from regulation. He invites you to love from overflow. So, this week, you will rise to the challenge of your assignment. It is the one designed for your healed heart, your restored rhythm, and your anchored soul.

And as you do, remember that crowns are not the reward for perfection. They are evidence of endurance. By the end of this week, you will not just be anchored. You will be activated.

DAY 36

You're Not Just Healing, You're Being Prepared

"Being confident of this, that He who began a good work in you will carry it on to completion until the day of Christ Jesus."
— Philippians 1:6 (NIV)

Healing. We have all experienced some measure of healing, both physically and emotionally. Today, let's look at it not so much as a destination, but rather as a divine preparation: it is the soil where new assignments begin to germinate.

I have learned that the seasons I once labeled waiting were actually planting.
God was planting what was needed to sustain my next season.
He was deepening discernment, expanding empathy,
and teaching me to tend what's unseen before celebrating what's grown.

There were many prayers, and every prayer was a seed.
Many tears and every tear, water.
Every pause, sunlight finding the soil of my heart.
God wasn't delaying the harvest; He was deepening my roots.
He was teaching me to trust His timing for transformation.

I began to see healing as a form of testimony. I discovered how faith and neuroscience work together to bring heart healing, how spiritual safety and nervous-system regulation are not opposites but allies.
He said we can be transformed by the renewing of our minds.
Healing the mind revealed how profoundly
the Spirit partners with biology to restore peace.

God is awakening what was already there.
The seeds of purpose were never lost; they were lying dormant,
Sometimes it's waiting for healing to create the right conditions to germinate.
God didn't plant something new in you;
He stirred to life what He placed there long ago:
the compassion, the insight, the resilience, the call.
Now, under the warmth of His presence,

what once felt buried begins to break through, a beautiful emergence.
For conversations that need your compassion.
For spaces that need your steadiness, your light.
For people who need your story to remind them that grace still works.
Now, under the warmth of His presence,
what once felt buried begins to break through into a beautiful emergence.
For conversations that need your compassion.
For spaces that need your steadiness, your light.
For people who need your story to remind them that grace still works.

God isn't just fixing you; He's forming you,
for something that needs your healed heart,
for someone who needs your more profound empathy,
your nervous-system wisdom, and your voice that's been tested in fire.

Your life will not be performance; it will be partnership.
You're being invited into the meaning of all your experiences.
Every boundary you've honored, every tear you've surrendered, every truth you've spoken is preparation. You're not behind. You're being built.

Whisper from God
"I'm not done with you, beloved.
Every slow step, every ache, every small "yes" I've used them all.
You are not stuck; you are in strategy.
I'm shaping strength beneath the surface.
Keep yielding. You are being prepared for good work."
— Love, God

DR. PATRICIA SAYS...

"Healing is a sacred apprenticeship. The process trains your nervous system for peace and your spirit for purpose. So your healing is not a delay my sister, you are in divine development. What's forming in you now will one day become shelter for others. So healing has never been wasted time. It's been growth and development. The sacred shaping of a vessel that could hold more light."

DAY 37

You Can Build from Here

"Unless the Lord builds the house, those who build it labor in vain."
— Psalm 127:1 (ESV)

There were seasons when my computer screen stayed open
late into the wee hours of the morning, notes scattered, ideas flowing
so quickly I'd text myself reminders before they slipped away.
Programs. Ministries. Messages.
Each one felt like a divine download waiting for its time.
Yet between teaching, leadership, family, and life's daily rhythm,
I'd look at those notes and whisper, *"Lord, what do I do with all this?"*

Over time, I learned something heavenly:
God never asked me to build everything at once.
He asked me to build from where I was. Right there.
When life felt full and my emotions ran deep,
I used to plan under pressure, rushing to make every idea tangible.
But healing taught me to build from peace instead.
When your heart is anchored, clarity naturally begins to rise.
You start to sense what's for now, what's for later,
and what's meant to rest in God's keeping.

Last summer, my husband and I built a small stoop together.
We thought it would be simple:
build the frame, pour the concrete, and be done.
But we quickly learned that before we could pour,
we had to dig a few inches down.
The foundation had to rest on solid ground,
deep enough to carry the weight of every foot that would step upon it.

That lesson stayed with me. Healing is like that, God teaching us to dig below the surface, strengthening what can't be seen so what's built above can carry the weight of purpose.
He doesn't rush the foundation because He intends for the house to last.

Every boundary you've honored, every "no" you've spoken in wisdom, every pause that allowed your heart to breathe, none of it is delay.
It's design.

Hey, don't rush it; you're being aligned.
You are not lost; you're being led.
And what's forming in this season will last
because it's being built from safety, not striving.
Let Him draw the blueprints.
Let peace be your foundation.
Let grace be your timeline.
You can build from here,
and this time,
what you build will last.

Whisper from God
"Beloved, I see the visions you've typed in quiet hours,
the ones waiting in your notes, glowing on your screen.
I see the thoughts in your heart, your dreams your hopes.
Don't mistake My pacing for postponement.
I'm teaching you to build with rest, not resistance.
The house will rise in its time, and when it does,
it will carry both your fingerprints and Mine."
— Love, God

DR. PATRICIA SAYS...
*"Healing is the art of sacred construction.
It's where the nervous system learns stability
so purpose can rest safely inside of you.
Build from your anchored self, not your anxious one—
because what's built in peace, lasts"*

DAY 38

The Rise Is Still Holy

"For the vision is yet for an appointed time... though it linger, wait for it; it will certainly come and will not delay."
— Habakkuk 2:3 (NIV)

After my husband and I finished pouring the stoop, we waited.
The surface looked dry long before it was ready,
but the concrete needed time to cure; to harden from the inside out.
It wasn't idle time; it was strengthening time.
And that's how God teaches us to rise.
Attempting to rise when we are internally weak
results in disaster.

There is a heavenly rhythm to becoming.
The path becomes known to us when we connect to Him,
and sometimes it's quiet.

Even Jesus' resurrection waited in silence for three days.
Nothing in the kingdom rushes maturity.
Even miracles can take their time.

The rise doesn't begin with applause;
it begins underground,
in the quiet setting of new strength,
in the unseen recalibration of a nervous system learning a new way.

When the body has lived too long in a hurry,
stillness feels foreign.
But slow isn't failure;
it's heaven's pacing.

This kind of rising happens without headlines.
It is measured not in miles but in mercy.
It's the tremor of courage returning to your chest,

the moment you stop holding your breath and realize
you can breathe again without fear.
You are not waiting for your life to begin;
you are being reintroduced to it, anew,
one regulated breath,
one surrendered "yes" at a time.

The same Spirit that steadied you in the breaking
is now anchoring you in becoming.
Heaven isn't impressed by speed;
it honors sustainability.

In the waiting, when your roots are deep,
your rise can be gentle and still be glorious.

So don't rush your resurrection.
Let it unfold like the morning light, beaming from the Son:
quiet, confident, unstoppable.

Whisper from God
"I see you rising, even when you can't feel it.
I see strength forming beneath your stillness.
Don't confuse rest for regression.
I'm not delaying you, I'm developing you.
Keep breathing, beloved.
The same power that raised My Son is raising you."
— Love, God

DR. PATRICIA SAYS...
*"The nervous system heals in rhythm, not in rush.
Every quiet recalibration is a resurrection rehearsal.
When peace feels possible again, you're witnessing a miracle in motion.
You are the evidence that slow miracles still happen,
and this rise is holy."*

DAY 39

You're Allowed to Feel Joy Again

"You turned my mourning into dancing; You removed my sackcloth and clothed me with joy"
— Psalm 30:11 (CSB)

For so long, joy felt like a risk.
After loss, after grief, after holding so much for so many,
the heart learns to brace for the next ache before it arrives.
Smiles can feel temporary. Laughter, borrowed.
The nervous system becomes fluent in survival, not celebration.

But healing rewrites that language.
It teaches the body that joy is not a trap, it's a teacher.
That happiness does not erase sorrow, but it redeems it.
That peace is not pretending its His presence.

The first time laughter rises after profound loss,
like after the passing of a beloved father or special friend,
it may sound strange, even like a betrayal.
Because resurrection always sounds strange to the grave.
That laughter is proof that mourning has met mercy.
That even in loss, life can still win; it is still winning!

Joy isn't a betrayal of what hurt you.
 It's the fruit of what has held you together all the time.
 It doesn't mean you've forgotten the pain;
 it means you've survived it without closing your heart.

The same power that steadied you in deep sorrow
 now calls you to lift your head and dance freely,
 not because everything in your life is perfect,
 but because the God who walked you through the valley
 is still present and taking you to the mountaintop.

Joy is holy resistance to what keeps you in the valley. It's your nervous system that's being rewired, like a neuronal revolt. Change is coming, my friend.
It says, "Grief will not have the final word."
It says, "Love still breathes here."
It says, "I'm alive, and that's my worship."

So go ahead, smile without suspicion.
Laugh without fear or apology.
Let the sunlight back in; feel the warmth
Joy is not the absence of pain; it's the evidence of His Presence.
God's presence, still here, still faithful, still healing.
Still saying, "I know the plans I have for you…"

Whisper from God
"Beloved, I delight in your delight.
I celebrate your joy.
You don't have to guard your gladness; give it freedom like the wind!
The same hands that caught your tears
are now teaching your heart to sing and dance again.
Let the laughter rise. It's safe now."
— Love, God

DR. PATRICIA SAYS...
"Joy is a nervous-system awakening. Its proof that safety has returned.
When you allow joy to coexist with your scars,
you become living evidence of God's resurrection power.
Even after loss, joy doesn't dishonor those you love; it echoes their
legacy. My mother's legacy, My sister's legacy!
You are not naive for smiling again, celebrating life.
You are brave for believing that light still belongs to you."

DAY 40

You've Been Crowned

"You crown the year with Your goodness, and Your paths drip with abundance"
— *Psalm 61:11 (NKJV)*

This is not the end of your story.
It is the moment you rise from the pages
radiant, regulated, and royal. You didn't just survive these forty days.
You were transformed in them.

You wept and were held. You questioned and were answered.
You broke and were rebuilt.
And through it all, the hand of God never trembled.
*He shaped your pain into purpose, your waiting into wisdom,
and your wounds into windows for His light to pour through.*

This is what healing looks like.
Not the absence of scars, but the beauty of knowing you've been redeemed.
Not a heart without history,
but one that beats in harmony with heaven again.
You didn't heal to go back to who you were.
You healed to remember who you've always been:
Chosen. Cherished. Crowned.

Every tear was an anointing oil.
Every boundary became a building block to glory!
Every "yes" you whispered in faith became another jewel in your crown.
This is what happens when a woman anchors herself in grace:
she discovers her glory.

You are not fragile; you are fortified with honor.
You are not forgotten, you are blessed and highly favored.
You are not striving anymore, you are standing gracefully,
'polished after the similitude of a palace,
crowned with peace, power and purpose.'

The journey didn't make you someone new.
It revealed the royalty that was hidden beneath your resilience all along.
You are the evidence that God still restores,
that healing is beautiful and holy,
that love will outlast loss everywhere and every time,
and that the shadow never wins the light!

So lift your head, beloved queen.
Acknowledge what God has done in you...and celebrate!
The same hands that held you through the storm
are now placing a crown of goodness, grace, and glory upon your head.
Walk in that truth. Worship in that truth.
And when the world asks how you made it,
Smile queen and tell them:
"God's grace held me. His truth healed me. His love crowned me."
This is your coronation moment, not because you're finished,
but because you are finally free and '**Restored to Royalty!!**'

Whisper from God
"*Daughter, I saw you in every midnight surrender.*
I heard you in every whispered prayer.
I watched you rebuild trust one trembling breath at a time.
You have not been overlooked. You have been overcome by My love.
I crown you with wisdom, with wonder,
and with peace that cannot be taken.
You are Mine. You are whole. You are crowned. You are Royal."
— Love, God

MY MOTHER WOULD SAY...
"*You can carry a crown and still lead with compassion.*
You can be powerful and still choose peace.
So walk with grace, speak with love, stand with dignity,
and rest like someone who is protected.
Let kindness be your strength, and peace be your armor.
You are God's daughter; no storm can cancel that.
Wear your crown with humility, and live your purpose with courage."
— Lady Grace Euline Hudson

A FINAL WORD FROM DR. PATRICIA

Thank you for allowing me to walk with you through these forty days of anchoring, healing, and restoration. My prayer is that you never forget this truth: God is not intimidated by your wounds. He meets you in the deep places, strengthens you in the quiet places, and restores you in the hidden places.

As you close this devotional, may you carry a steady confidence in your spirit...the confidence that comes from knowing you are held, seen, and deeply loved by a God who will never let you go. When life pulls, return to your anchor. When shame whispers, return to your anchor. When hope rises, return to your anchor and rise with it.

If this journey has blessed you, I invite you to continue through the Anchored Soul Companion Journal and the resources of the Dr. Patricia Wellness Collective. There is more healing ahead, and you do not have to walk it alone.

Stay anchored. Stay hopeful. Stay held.

Dr. Patricia Hudson-Henry

WAYS TO USE THE ANCHORED SOUL DEVOTIONAL + JOURNAL

The Anchored Soul is not just a devotional. It is a rhythm, a sanctuary, and a soul-restoring practice. And the journal is where healing becomes personal, as you can explore and intentionally apply the material to your life. Here are creative and sacred ways to use both:

Prayer Meetings
Turn prayer time into a soul-calming encounter.
- Open with one devotional day as your "centering moment."
- Allow two minutes of silence for breathing and nervous-system settling.
- Have participants journal a simple phrase: "Where did God meet me today?"
- End with a united prayer of anchoring: "Lord, steady our hearts."

Women's Ministries Gatherings
Create a warm, reflective circle of sisterhood.
- Choose one devotional day as the theme for the evening.
- Allow each woman to write her grounding prompt privately before sharing.
- Invite a testimony about how God is settling emotions or rewriting old narratives.
- Close by speaking life over one another: "You are safe here."

Small Groups
Turn your group into a community of anchored hearts.
- Assign one devotional day each week.
- Begin by journaling in silence for five minutes.
- Use the Heart Prompt as a conversation starter.
- Create a ritual: end each week by praying over shared journal prompt responses.

Bible Study Circles
Let Scripture do its healing work.
- Start with the Scripture Anchor and trace it through multiple translations.
- Ask: "What happens in my body when I read this?"
- Journal any shifts in emotion, posture, breath, or clarity.
- Allow Scripture + journaling to become a neurospiritual practice.

WAYS TO USE THE ANCHORED SOUL DEVOTIONAL + JOURNAL

Wellness or Healing Retreats
Create a retreat experience that integrates faith and neuroscience.
- Open each session with one devotional day and a grounding breath.
- Use journaling time as guided emotional processing.
- Pair journal prompts with movement: stretching, walking, gentle yoga, or silence.
- End with a community ritual: tearing up old narratives or speaking affirmations.

Support Groups
Create a safe, non-judgmental healing space.
- Read the devotional aloud and pause for reflection.
- Allow individuals to journal feelings instead of speaking if talking is too hard.
- Invite optional sharing using phrases like: "What felt true for you today?"
- Close by returning to the Whisper from God together.

Sisterhood Circles
Build bonding, belonging, and emotional safety.
- Begin with the Whisper from God, spoken aloud by one woman.
- Let everyone journal their response before sharing.
- Use the Stretch Prompt to deepen vulnerability gently.
- End with a "royalty affirmation": "You are anchored, anointed, and held."

Grief or Restoration Ministries
Hold space for sorrow with tenderness.
- Choose gentle devotional days like the ones on shame, grief, and peace.
- Let journaling be silent, spacious, and unhurried.
- Encourage participants to write letters to God, to loved ones, or to their future selves.
- Close with a grounding ritual such as holding warm tea, touching their heart, or lighting a candle.

CONNECT WITH DR. PATRICIA

Thank you for allowing me to walk with you through these forty days. If this devotional has touched your heart, I would love to stay connected with you.

STAY CONNECTED
Website: DrPatriciaWellnessCollective.com
Email: info@DrPatriciaWellnessCollective.com
YouTube: Dr. Patricia Wellness Collective
Instagram: @DrPatriciaWellnessCollective
Facebook: The Anchored Soul Community

FOR SPEAKING AND MINISTRY INVITATIONS
Women's Ministries Retreats
Prayer and Healing Gatherings
Neuroscience and Faith Workshops
Mental Health and Emotional Wellness Events
Church and Leadership Trainings
Join the Anchor Community

Scan the QR code to join the Anchored Soul online community for teachings, encouragement, and live sessions designed to help you stay grounded, safe, and spiritually steady.

Your journey matters. Your healing matters.
And I am honored to walk beside you.

Dr. Patricia Hudson-Henry

ABOUT THE AUTHOR

Dr. Patricia Hudson-Henry is a Professor and the Founder & Visionary of the Dr. Patricia Wellness Collective, home to her signature programs—PACERS Parenting™, Heart & Mind Connection™, Couples Clinic HQ™, Restore Your Royalty™, Healthy Mentality Network™, C-Suite Synergy, and Big Feeling Brave Hearts™. She is known for her unique blend of faith-led insight, therapeutic clarity, compassionate presence, and neuroscience. Her doctorate in clinical psychology with an emphasis in neuropsychology strengthens her understanding of the intimate connection between neuroscience and faith.

For more than 20 years, Dr. Patricia has served in clinical and leadership roles—including Deputy Director of Psychology at a state forensic psychiatric hospital and Assistant Clinical Director at a Partial Hospitalization Program — supporting adolescents and adults with complex emotional needs. As a university educator, she teaches psychology and sociology, shaping the next generation of mental health professionals with both scientific rigor and spiritual grounding.

She is a sought-after speaker for seminars, retreats, conferences, and ministry events, offering transformative teaching rooted in emotional safety, identity, resilience, and spiritual restoration. Her curriculum development and wellness programs have reached classrooms, churches, families, and communities worldwide.

Dr. Patricia is married to Ricardo Henry, and together they have three children: Ife Grace, Elle-Michelle Nina, and Prince Ricardo, who continually inspire her work and faith. She honors her mother, Grace Euline Hudson (née Lewis), whose gentle consistency, warmth, and sacrificial love shaped her earliest sense of safety and profoundly influenced the healing work she now shares with others.

Through her writing, teaching, and therapeutic ministry, Dr. Patricia creates sacred spaces where the overwhelmed can breathe, the wounded can heal, and every heart can rediscover the God who anchors and restores.

www.ingramcontent.com/pod-product-compliance
Lightning Source LLC
Chambersburg PA
CBHW050914160426
43194CB00011B/2399